THE BOY
WITH ONLY
ONE SHOE

IN SUPPORT OF ● Royal Air Force Benevolent Fund

THE BOY WITH ONLY ONE SHOE

An illustrated memoir of wartime life with
Bomber Command

WARRANT OFFICER (RET.)

JOHN HENRY MELLER
WITH CAROLINE BROWNBILL

This book is a memoir, based on a mix of recollection and historical fact. The
authors tried to recreate events, locales and conversations from memories of them.
For reasons of discretion, in some instances the authors have changed the names of
individuals and places, They may also have changed some identifying characteristics
and details such as physical properties, occupations and places of residence.

ISBN: 978-1-8380467-0-5

Published by John Henry Meller and Caroline Brownbill.

All original photography and documents © John Henry Meller

Editor: Claire Sanders / clairesanders.uk

Cover design, illustration and interior formatting:
Mark Thomas / Coverness.com

Table of Contents

INTRODUCTION

John Henry Meller served as aircrew in Bomber Command during World War 2. At the time of writing, John is 95 years of age and lives with his wife Barbara, 92. They recently celebrated their 71st wedding anniversary and live with their daughter Caroline, son-in-law Jamie and granddaughter Stephanie on their small holding near Cardiff in South Wales.

John writes:

My son-in-law Jamie persuaded me to write these memoirs for Stephanie so that she would be able to appreciate how much we owe to those who fought against the odds to defend our country, our world and our freedom. The ordeals endured by my generation, not only affected the outcome of World War 2, but also altered our way of life, our values and our expectations forever. In particular women were given the opportunity to prove beyond all doubt, both to themselves and others, their capabilities, bravery and self-worth in all occupations and professions.

FOREWORD

HEAVEN CAN WAIT

My mother held me close to her; I was just three years old and she was terrified that I wouldn't come out of my coma. The doctor warned my parents of the severity of my condition. Our daily help had been preparing a bath for me. She had already poured the boiling water into the zinc bath and was in the process of collecting cold water to add to it, but in the meantime, I had clambered in unsupervised. I sustained third degree burns to my lower back and the shock to my tiny body was immense.

As the doctor and my parents looked helplessly at my frail body I started to stir and whimper. They listened closely and heard me say: "The angel wouldn't let me in." It started as a murmur but I kept repeating it over and over again and getting more and more upset: "The angel wouldn't let me in."

Later when I had regained more strength I spoke more about my experience. I had followed a glowing light up some stairs, climbing higher and higher far above the clouds. Just as it was getting too steep to climb any further; a figure appeared, standing just inside some partially open gates. I looked up at this heavenly being, and he looked down at my feet and said: "You can't come in - because you only have one shoe."

The apparition and the gateway then just faded away.

My parents often spoke of the angel and my lost shoe story to friends and relatives. I can remember my mother telling everyone she thought I must have a guardian angel and my uncle wondering about how many close shaves I would have in my lifetime. He added that at least I wouldn't have to suffer all the horrors young men experienced in the Great War. With that he patted me on the head and said: "I'd stick to the ground young man - don't go soaring up into the sky again."

I can still remember that moment and the immense sadness that I felt as the angel drifted away. The scars are still visible on my body some 92 years later, but I am glad to say that I still haven't found that other shoe!

CHAPTER 1

MY EARLY CHILDHOOD

During my early childhood my family lived in Winwick Street, Warrington, England. Ours was a terraced house with a tobacconist shop fronting on to the street, owned and run by my mother. We were in the middle of a small row of shops, to the left of us was an ice cream shop, on the other side was a sweet shop and next-door to that was a greengrocer. Each shop was licensed to sell a restricted range of items and could not stock the same goods as another shop in the vicinity. This rule was implemented to maintain a reasonable profit margin for shopkeepers and to encourage more entrepreneurs into retail.

Warrington had originally been a small market town, but the 19th century industrial expansion had increased Warrington's population to just over 65,000. The main forms of industry near us were metal foundries, particularly iron and aluminium and tanneries - we had a large tannery opposite us. In the 1920s small retail shops like ours were an expanding industry.

My mother, Ada Meller was an excellent entrepreneur and an extremely liberated woman for that era, as she earned her own income and was very much in charge of her own shop. She worked very long hours, from 5am until 8pm, and managed to juggle looking after three young children and running a household.

My mother was extremely lucky to have a young girl called Hilda Houghton to help her with the daily chores. Hilda had walked into the shop one day and explained that she had just left school, (school leaving age at the time was 14 years), and was urgently seeking domestic work. Initially, my mother explained that whilst that would be helpful, she didn't have sufficient funds to employ anyone. Finding any employment, particularly for a young girl, was extremely difficult at that time and Hilda told my mother that any income would be better than nothing, so my mother agreed to visit her parents to discuss it with them. Shortly afterwards Hilda started working for us on a daily basis from 8am until 8pm, (including Sundays), for a very small amount of pay, but with as many benefits as my mother was able to add to the arrangement, such as any cast-off clothing, surplus food, plus a two penny packet of Woodbine cigarettes for her father every day. I remember her father, as he had been seriously injured both physically and mentally whilst fighting as a soldier in France during World War 1. Every time the subject of Hilda's father was brought up in our household, my father would angrily denounce the government and state how poorly they had all been treated since returning from the war.

My father, Herbert Meller, was a foot soldier with the Lancashire Fusiliers and my uncle Ernie was in the cavalry. They would often discuss not only the horrors they had witnessed during the war but equally the injustice they had felt on returning home. My father used to say that they had been promised a hero's return to a "Land of Hope and Glory", but instead, they came home to poverty and unemployment. My father was lucky as he had his own butcher's shop and my mother's business to return to, but most had nothing. As a result, my parents did their best to help Hilda's father by sending him his tobacco and giving a bit of meagre but valued employment to his daughter.

I can't imagine how my mother ever coped before Hilda came to work for her. Hilda worked long hours and was hard working by nature, but, occasionally, we would go looking for her and find her fast asleep, on the chaise longue in our front parlour. My mother, who was a stickler for hard work, acknowledged that this young scrap of a girl desperately needed a little rest and would tell us to leave her to sleep.

Hilda washed all our clothes by hand as washing machines had yet to be invented. The clothes were first scrubbed on a washboard then partly dried by squeezing water out through the rollers of a mangle before being hung to dry. Certain items of clothing were pressed using a heavy moulded piece of iron with a handle on it, which you heated on the kitchen stove. It was usual to have two irons, one in use and the other pre-heating on the stove.

My mother made sure the kitchen stove was lit every day of the year. She would get up early in order to have the shop open by 5am to accommodate all the factory workers as they set off for work, which started at 6am prompt. Hilda would then tend to the stove throughout the day. Hanging on the wall beside the fireplace was a set of bellows to blow air into the dying embers to set the fire ablaze again. The stove had an open grate with a built-in oven on one side in which our meals were cooked. The top of the stove was used for saucepans and there was always a kettle on the boil to make visitors or home-comers a welcoming cup of tea.

The larder, where all the food was kept, had a window frame, but instead of a pane of glass the frame was covered with wire-mesh gauze to allow air to circulate and to keep insects out. Meat was hung up on hooks attached to the ceiling. If the weather got hot a block of ice, delivered from my father's butchers' shop, would be placed in a container in the larder to keep it cool. Fridges and freezers had not yet been invented.

Hilda would often ask me to help her collect the milk. To do this we would fetch a large jug and go and stand outside in the street, in front of the shop, and wait for the horse-drawn cart containing a large twenty-gallon milk churn to arrive.

The milkman was the farmer from the local dairy farm; he would get up early to milk the cows and then set off on his rounds to sell it. He would see us waiting with our jug and get his horse to stop right outside our door. I loved stroking the soft muzzle of the horse while I waited for our milk. The milkman had a long-handled ladle, which held exactly one pint of milk; once measured, he would pour it into our jug for us.

I liked watching the greengrocer, (two shops down from us), loading his fruit and vegetables onto a cart. It was a mobile shop that he took all around Warrington selling fresh produce. My father always admired the grocer's horse, and said it was too good to be doing the grocery rounds - it was a very handsome black gelding called Bobby. The horse seemed very happy in his task though and was often given a treat of a bruised apple or slightly wilted lettuce. The grocer's cart always looked a splendid sight with all the items set out beautifully. Fortunately, Bobby wasn't the type to bolt off and upturn the cart, and he did look magnificent pulling it – my father said he even put some of the carriage horses to shame.

In stark contrast was the heavy plod of the rag-and-bone man's horse that lumbered down the street. The rag-and-bone man collected any bones (mainly used to make glue) and spare rags or clothes. We used to give him our Sunday best once we had outgrown them and for this we would be given the magnificent gift of a goldfish in a jam jar. We soon had a small aquarium occupied by the fish we had collected from the clothes we'd exchanged!

It was never dull in the street outside our shop as there was always something interesting happening, with costermongers passing by, all calling out their services for sale; everything from chimney sweeps with all their brushes in a trolley, to shoe repair and knife sharpening. Directly outside our shop there was often a man operating a barrel organ with a pet monkey sitting on his shoulder. Whenever I saw him arrive, I would dash into the shop and shout: "Mum the man with the monkey is here!" My mother would then give me a half penny to put in his hat for which he always thanked us. He kept playing but would always turn around with a lovely big grin on his face.

Mealtimes were always an important part of our family life - our mother would do all the cooking while Hilda prepared the table. We always dined at home sitting as a family with Hilda included - we were never allowed to leave the table until we were told to do so by our mother. We didn't eat anything between meals as snack foods didn't really exist. Hilda was given any surplus food to take home for her family.

It was an era when very few homes had bathrooms; we certainly didn't know anyone with a bathroom or a plumbed-in toilet as there were no sewers in our local area. Every member of our family bathed in a zinc bath in front of a blazing fire, the boiling hot water having been obtained from a copper – a vessel that was also used to boil clothes. The copper was kept in the scullery where a brick-built boiler was lit every Friday. I loved bath night, the firelight and the crackling of the flames was so relaxing and the zinc bath kept the water hot for ages.

The towels were draped over the fireguard to keep them nice and warm for when you got out.

Our toilet was outside at the far end of our backyard and was emptied regularly by council workers who could access the yard from a side road. We had a chamber pot under our beds to save us a trip out to the yard in the night, but poor Hilda had the horrible task of emptying the chamber pots so always encouraged us to go last thing before bedtime. It was a horrible run out to the toilet in the rain and the cold.

Each of the three bedrooms in our house had a washstand with an ewer and a basin. Lukewarm water was carried upstairs and Hilda would later pour the used washing water into a bucket and carry it downstairs to empty it. The washbasin came as part of a set that included a soap dish, water jug, slop pale and chamber pot all in the same decorative design.

Our beds were so comfortable; the mattresses, eiderdowns and pillows were filled with duck down feathers that just moulded around you and were so snug and warm. During the winter the bedrooms could at times get very cold, with the windows completely frosted over with icicles dangling down inside as well as outside, but once I was snuggled into my duck down mattress, I didn't seem to notice the cold, although it was horrible getting out of bed. I would try to get dressed by pulling my clothes under the covers and sliding into them.

During particularly chilly weather my mother would put extra woollen blankets on our beds and at least one stone hot water bottle beneath the sheet and place my flannelette pyjamas on it to warm them up. I always remember my bed being so snug and warm.

I can still remember the routine morning sounds that I would listen to from the comfort of my bed. The room where I slept had a window overlooking the main street below from which I could hear the "knocker up", (a man employed for a small fee, who carried a specially made, lightweight, very long pole that he used to tap on the bedroom windows of those desperate not to sleep in and miss a day's work) - very few people could afford a clock. He started his rounds at about 5am. Next, I would hear the "lamp lighter" shuffling along the pavement putting out the flame of each gas street lamp that he had lit with a long pole the previous evening.

A while later I would start to hear the workers' wooden clogs on the streets as they started to make their way into the local factories and the tannery which was opposite our shop. Factory workers all tended to wear wooden clogs, as they were hard wearing as well as offering good industrial protection. The clip-clop of the clogs would steadily increase until there was a whole army of workers that would quickly subside to a trickle. This was followed by the tannery and factory sirens warning that 6am was soon approaching; that was swiftly followed by the frantic clatter of those who had slept-in as they rushed towards their place of employment, desperate to get there before the 6am lock-out. At 6am, prompt, the gates were locked and anyone who failed to make it in time would lose their day's work to one of the unemployed men waiting in the queue outside the gate. Through my window I would see men gathering in an orderly queue from early morning, irrespective of the weather conditions, just in case they could get work if any of the regular workers failed to turn up due to sickness or being tardy. It was very sad watching them being turned away. Even as a child I was aware that there was a lot of poverty, yet despite this cash from the shop was kept in an unlocked drawer behind the counter. There were no tills or safes and no one would contemplate that someone might try to steal the money.

My mother was kept very busy in the shop not only with matters of retail, but also as a trusted member of the community. She was often called on for advice and a shoulder to cry on by many of her customers. I can remember overhearing her offering comfort to a regular customer whose husband was employed as a local factory worker. The lady explained how he, along with all the other factory employees, had to go to the local pub to collect their wages. It was expected that they would stay and treat the foreman and give him a "sweetener", which they had to do to preserve their employment. This was just an unwritten rule. They consequently went home with very little money remaining. Women were not allowed in public houses so couldn't enter to encourage their husbands to leave. My mother suggested that she do what a few of the bolder wives did, which was to wait outside for their husbands to arrive and insist on staying there until they brought them some of their wages.

Years later some public houses introduced a private

lounge which ladies could be invited into as long as they were accompanied by their husband or father, but they were still not allowed into the public bar. It wasn't until 1982 that a new law was passed finally permitting a woman to enter a public house without a male chaperone and buy herself a drink.

CHAPTER 2

CAT-O'-NINE TAILS

In spite of being victorious in the Great War, Great Britain's economy was suffering and poverty was everywhere. Thanks to poor education and a lack of access to contraceptives, many families had as many as ten children. Very few women had paid work as it was expected that they would get married and then be too busy running the household and bringing up children. They were expected to have a meal waiting for their husband on his return home from work. If there was insufficient food for all the family it was often the woman who would go without a full meal in order to ensure that her husband and children were fed.

Despite the level of poverty, there appeared to be little fear or worry about crime such as robbery, burglary or shoplifting.

This was possibly because most people were born, lived and died in the same neighbourhood and were family and community orientated; they all knew and respected each other and the local policeman. It was expected that everyone would help one another as you never knew when you might need help yourself. The consequences of offending and being rejected by your community and family were a huge deterrent to committing a crime.

As children we were allowed to go for walks under the supervision of my older sister. In our area there were no semi-detached or detached properties - every street was terraced either with shop fronts or just streets of terraced housing. A few of these properties, (such as ours), were larger, but most comprised just two bedrooms upstairs and a living room and kitchen with a stove downstairs. A great many houses didn't have any form of lighting other than the light from the fire plus a few candles. Some people invested in oil lamps and those who could afford to up-graded their homes to include gas lighting; the majority, however, still used candles.

Women would often sit outside their front doors, (when the weather was fine), knitting, sewing or darning clothes. Most people wore clothes that were much mended, darned and washed out, as they didn't have the money to replace them, but they still took immense pride in their appearance. Most young girls learned how to sew and both make and repair clothes. Most people of all ages tried to keep an outfit as their Sunday best, used only to attend church or for other very special occasions.

I still find the fashion of ripped clothing very strange, as even the poorest families would darn their clothes and would never dream of being seen with a tear. Ripped clothing was the ultimate in deprivation as it indicated that you were so poor you didn't have the means to mend your clothing or the pride in oneself to care and were only one step away from the workhouse. I can remember the first time I saw my first fashionably ripped jeans. I caught a train to London; it stopped at a station and a young woman got on wearing a pair of jeans that were torn on both knees. I felt so sorry for her as there was no attempt to patch them. I then looked at her overall appearance and noted that she looked well fed, clean and otherwise presentable so concluded that she must have taken a fall. It was some time later that I realised these rips were not accidental or due to poverty, but a deliberate fashion statement. I was aghast.

There was a Cottage Home near us, which my mother explained was for children who had been orphaned or whose parents were unable to look after them. We tended to avoid going near the Cottage Home as it made us feel so sad. I can remember walking past the Warrington Workhouse one day with my brother and sister. We were very upset by what we saw and walked away in a stunned, shocked silence, glancing at one another for reassurance. There were haunted looking people of all ages, from children our age all the way to the elderly. The children belonged to parents who were also in the workhouse and seeing them made me shudder - we couldn't get away from there fast enough! I can remember a short while later overhearing a conversation between my mother and a customer in our shop, saying how it was good to hear that the local authority had decided to spend some money on improving the conditions. Not long after that the workhouse became the Warrington District Hospital. I can still see those poor, grey figures and I always hoped that conditions did indeed improve for them.

I started school at the age of five. Although my mother took me along to be registered it was my sister, Cissie, who actually took me to school from my very first day as my parents were fully occupied running their businesses. I still remember being taken to the headmaster's office on that first day to have my introductory welcome. He was an elderly man with a stern face who peered over his desk at me. I was left in no doubt that I was there to learn and to do that I had to concentrate which meant I had to listen and be good. He then pointed to a cat-o-nine tails, (a whip made of nine lines of cord), which was hanging on a hook behind his office door, and said: "That is for flogging the children who are not good". There was also a long cane displayed on the front of his desk. Whilst I don't believe that the whip ever left its hook, the cane was most definitely used - on those who needed to be "reminded".

The deterrent appeared to be very effective. There is no doubt that as youngsters our characters are shaped by what we are taught at home by our parents, and at school by our teachers. Discipline was very strict but, to my mind, fair. Disruptive pupils, truants and bullies were suitably punished.

If we stepped out of line our parents, teachers, relatives, friends and even strangers would have no hesitation in chastising us. The police would readily apprehend anyone, whatever age, caught breaking the law or using insulting words or behaviour. We were taught to respect our parents, teachers, elders and all people in authority.

It wasn't until I was at school that I started to learn about people from other parts of the world. Whilst we take our multi-cultural society for granted now, world travel was a much greater task then than it is today and the whole subject sounded extremely exotic to me. Of course, I realise now that there were plenty of people from other countries living in Great Britain during that period in our history, particularly near the ports and big cities, but my young eyes had never seen a person of colour other than the pictures in those schoolbooks.

Then, as now, we wrote in pencil at first but, as we progressed, we were allowed to use a pen. The big difference was that the pen had a nib that was dipped into an inkwell on our desks and we each had a sheet of blotting paper to dry excess ink. We had to be very careful not to drop blots onto the paper or elsewhere, or smudge the writing, otherwise we were told off and would lose marks. Too many blots would be considered a lack of concentration and could result in a visit to the headmaster's office.

We had to walk about half a mile to and from school whatever the weather; even for our mid-day meal, (there were no school meals or option to take a packed lunch). The school day wasn't that far removed from that of today - starting at 9am and finishing at 4pm with a mid-day break and a short break between lessons during the morning and afternoon. There was no school transport or parents waiting outside the school gates. There were no pedestrian crossings, traffic lights, school-crossing patrols or any markings on the roads. Traffic normally travelled at a slow pace therefore there was no need for speed signs.

During the winter months we would occasionally get lost on the way home due to the thick smog caused by the smoke from all the coal fires mixing with dense fog. It would start off as an exciting challenge, but would often end with all three of us clinging together, making our way along the house walls and shop fronts by touch, feeling lost and not a little scared. It was very dangerous to cross the roads in those conditions, but at least they tended to be fairly deserted during the smog. I can remember the great relief when we reached home. The smog could be so dense it would have been futile for our parents or anyone else to try and meet us and, as strange as it may seem now, we did not expect them to.

We did have to cross one very wide main road to get to school, which at times could be very busy. We were instructed to wait until we could see an adult who was about to cross and ask them to assist us. The stranger would take us by the hand and see us safely across the road.

The traffic in those days mainly consisted of horses pulling carts, pedlars and hawkers or rag-and-bone men pushing carts and grinding machines; on rare occasions we might see a motorcycle, a car or even a coal-fired lorry! During the summer months there would be ice cream sellers riding tricycles with a coolant box in front, full of ice creams.

One day we couldn't find an adult to help us cross the road and decided to give it a go on our own. I gave a cursory check of the traffic and started to cross. A few steps in, there was a loud bang and a great deal of pain - I quickly came to on the ground, but was aware that I had injured my shoulder. I had been knocked over by a motorcyclist who was overtaking a horse-drawn cart. The motorcyclist took us into the school and explained to a teacher what had happened. My arm was put in a sling and I was sent back to class, but I was in a great deal of pain all afternoon. Back then there was no National Health Service (NHS) – therefore you had to pay for all medical treatment so, despite the pain I was suffering, my teacher was reluctant to call a doctor. When I got home my mother was appalled and immediately took me to see our family doctor who treated me for a dislocated shoulder. Although both our parents were kept very busy running their businesses, as children, we always felt loved and cared for. Whenever we were ill my mother would pay for us to see a doctor, but I can remember children in school getting ill or even breaking a limb and their parents not being able to afford to pay for medical care. The majority of women in our neighbourhood had to cope with childbirth at home with just the help of other family members.

Fortunately, my shoulder quickly recovered, but our mother

was still very annoyed at us for crossing the road on our own. She did admit though that I had been incredibly unlucky to be knocked over by a motorcycle. They were still a relative rarity, despite more appearing on our roads year by year.

At that time, owners of motor vehicles had to be fairly mechanically minded as there were very few mechanics or workshops around. Fortunately, the vehicles' engineering was fairly basic. There were no indicators - you just stuck your arm out if turning right and rotated your arm if turning left; there were no interior lights, radios, seat belts, heaters or rear-view mirrors. You had a rubber horn that you squeezed to beep. Most tyres were made from solid rubber so there were never any punctures. Vehicles didn't have keys, you just had to put the starter handle in and crank the engine over by hand until it fired. The starter handle was always particularly difficult to turn when the weather was cold, with the engine backfiring and the handle having to be turned again.

If ever you saw a broken down vehicle it would soon be surrounded by passers-by, wishing to sound knowledgeable on such matters, suggesting cleaning the spark plugs or offering to check or top up the oil or water.

Motor vehicles had no servicing schedules, no MOTs and there were no such things as driving tests or lessons. You just got a friend or a relative to teach you and, to be honest, more time was spent teaching you how to start, service and fix the vehicle when it broke down than on driving techniques. Despite this there were few accidents as there was so little traffic. If you came upon a traffic jam it was more likely to be caused by some horse-related issue; lameness, disobedience or by one panicking and bolting, spilling the contents of its cart as it went. Sometimes, particularly in the evenings, we would see a horse pulling a cart and the driver asleep, (or possibly drunk!), but the horse knew its own way home.

As children we loved to see the huge Shire horses pulling the dray full of beer barrels on its delivery round from the local brewery. One of our uncles drove a dray and whenever we saw him, we would wave as he passed and think how nice it would be to sit there in charge of those magnificent horses. The reality of it though was that our uncle had very little spare time to himself. As soon as he got back to the depot he would have to see to the unloading of the dray, attend to the horses and to the large amounts of harness, some of which he would take home to clean. Whenever we stayed with our cousins, we would all spend the evening cleaning the horses' tack and polishing the numerous brasses that adorned the harness.

We always looked forward to May Day, (1st May) also known as Walking Day, as there were always lots of street celebrations and a parade with decorated horse-drawn carts which you could ride in or you could just join in by following the band. Everyone dressed up in their Sunday best and the streets were full of excited people, all happy to have the day off work and school. One of my favourite childhood photographs was taken on May Day, with the three of us children standing on the front doorstep of our shop.

Sometimes after school, before going home, we would walk up to visit the abattoir in the hope of seeing our father who, as a butcher, was often there buying carcasses ready to cut into joints back at his shop. We were allowed to just wander in and would watch aghast but morbidly fascinated. It was not a pleasant sight, but no one thought to protect us from it - in fact, quite the opposite. It was seen as an important part of growing up, as if you wanted to eat meat then you should know how it arrived on your plate. We were not allowed to waste a scrap of meat, partly because of the expense but, just as importantly, because an animal had died so we could eat and it would be disrespectful to that animal to waste it.

At weekends our parents allowed us to go out for the full day exploring - seemingly without any fear for our safety. Each day was a day of learning, of freedom, of exercise and, sometimes, of adventure. On one such occasion we decided to go and explore the area called Burtonwood, approximately a four-mile walk from our house. There, we enjoyed picking blackberries along the hedgerows and watching different types of birds, foxes and rabbits running about in the fields and nearby woodland. Little did we know that this whole area would soon become a wartime air force base, that one day I would be employed there and that Cissie would meet her future American husband there also.

We had just started to retrace our steps home when we were startled by flashes of lightning and the threatening rumble of thunder. When the rain started, it absolutely poured down so we started to run, desperately seeking some form of shelter.

As we ran, we came across a partially open garden gate with a large tree just inside the garden. Without giving it any thought we all ran to shelter underneath the overhanging branches. We had not been there long when a very kind lady holding an umbrella came running from the house and told us to follow her. She took us indoors and into her front parlour where she settled us down in front of a blazing fire and brought us all a cup of tea and a cake. She then came and sat down in a chair next to us and asked us our names and where we lived and then, very patiently, explained the folly of standing under a tree in a thunderstorm. We hadn't realised the terrible danger of being struck by lightning. We spent a few happy hours in her company, chatting and getting warm and dry whilst the storm passed overhead. By the time the storm had abated we realised we didn't have much daylight left. We thanked the lady and hurried as fast as we could to reach home just as night fell. Darkness was fast approaching as we came racing around the corner of our street. Our mother was standing outside the shop waiting for us and I can still see the worried look on her face.

The next day, the same lady visited our home to check we had arrived home safely. My mother was delighted to meet her and welcomed her in for tea. Whenever we had visitors my mother always took them into the front room for tea and cakes. I can remember that we had a very large aspidistra plant in our front room, which thrived on the tea dregs that my mother always poured into its bowl once our guests had left. Aspidistras were a very popular houseplant during this period as they coped with the gas fumes and required little attention.

It was nice to see the lady again and thank her for her kindness. We always intended to go back and see her another day but rarely ventured that far from home again.

Occasionally we would go and see a lantern show - a series of camera slides with someone giving a running commentary. One of the most memorable shows was *The Sinking of the Titanic*. Although she sank on 14th April 1912, over a decade later, there was still a palpable disbelief that such a tragedy had occurred on the ship's maiden voyage. The commentator explained the errors that had led to the tragedy; most of the passengers who survived were women although many stayed on board as they refused to leave their loved ones. Lack of lifeboats and inadequate staff training meant that 1,522 people perished. It was incredibly sobering. The entry fee to these shows was two clean jam jars!

Sundays were our only real family day, and were all about church and lunch. As children it was Sunday school and, when we got older, the church service itself. At the time there were strict dress codes for all. The ladies had to wear hats and the gentlemen had to remove theirs before entering the church - and all observed. Church over, it was back home for a real highlight - a roast beef dinner! Whilst we were lucky enough to be well fed with varied, tasty meals throughout the week, the Sunday roast was still very much a treat and just the fuel to prepare us for another working week.

CHAPTER 3

ESCAPE TO THE COUNTRY

When I was eight, we moved into a bungalow in the country near Padgate, which is five miles to the east of Warrington. My parents kept their shops, but by then they had greatly reduced the shop opening hours; Hilda was still a great help to my mother. The bungalow had some land with a pond on which we kept a small rowing boat. It also had a small paddock that we soon put to use. I can still remember all the excitement the day my father returned home with a small bay pony led by a piece of rope. My father had been at the abattoir when someone had brought the pony in for slaughter as it only had one eye. My father had taken pity on it and decided to bring it home to live in our paddock and for us to learn to ride on it. As the pony only had one eye, we decided to call him "Oner". I don't think any of us particularly learnt to ride on Oner but we did enjoy running around the field with him and giving him titbits. Occasionally one of us would be brave enough to sit on him, but we didn't have any tack so just clambered on bare back.

When we moved, we had to change to a different school. Our new school was Padgate Church of England School (which has now been renamed Christ Church Cof E School). The school was about two miles from our house, which was too long a walk to go home for our mid-day break so every day we went to the local fish and chip shop and bought a pennyworth of chips and a two-penny fish for our lunch. We all loved chips and we had them most days with our meals at home as well.

As my parents still worked long hours in their shops in Warrington, it was normal to arrive home to an empty house, but the front door was always unlocked, so we could let ourselves in. There was no thought about being burgled despite all the unemployment and poverty. As there was no rush to get home, we would normally go to the local recreation ground and play on the swings, the roundabout and the seesaw, or play football, rugby, cricket, leap frog or tick.

Once a week after school a group of us travelled by train, from Padgate to Warrington, where we attended the swimming baths. We were taught all of the different swimming strokes, life saving and the art of resuscitation. We didn't have a shower at home, so really enjoyed the pleasure of showering at the baths before and after the swimming lessons. On our way home from the swimming baths, we would always visit a nearby cake shop, where those who could afford it would purchase a halfpenny Wet Nelly. This was a delicious rich form of bread pudding. The portions were really large, so those of us who could afford to buy them always shared a section with those who couldn't.

The train was powered by steam, and operated by a driver and a stoker who would keep the fire hot enough to boil the water to make the steam. I remember thinking I'd rather be the engine driver than the stoker, as the stoker was responsible for replenishing the coal and the water from the depots, situated near the stations. It was fascinating watching these men working as one with this beast of a machine.

It didn't take us long to find a short cut across the fields to and from our house to school and we soon grew to love this walk. As the three of us strolled through the countryside we would play games such as "I spy", or would see who could be the first to name all the different kinds of crops being cultivated such as wheat, barley, corn, carrots, swedes, turnips, potatoes, mustard and peas. We would have competitions to see who would be the first to notice wild flowers as they came into bloom, and who could name them. The ones we didn't know we would either take to school and ask the teacher, or take them home to ask our parents. We would also see who could be the first to see wild animals such as rabbits, hares, slow worms and grass snakes, different types of insects, honey bees, bumble bees, dragonflies, gnats and butterflies.

On our way home we would visit a particular pond and I

can remember how taken we were when we first saw a jelly-like string of eggs floating on top of the water. Each day we would be excited to return to see how the eggs were developing, until finally, much to our excitement, they turned into tadpoles. I can still hear our excited chatter and remember the enthusiasm we had for our journey home, the ever-changing countryside and the cycle of the seasons. Our days were highlighted by events such as our tadpoles losing their tails, or the sighting of a stickleback, a kingfisher or a dragonfly. I remember the day that we could hardly navigate our way to the pond for fear of treading on one of our baby frogs as they made their way from the pond into the hedgerows. Each year we would watch in readiness for the frogspawn to appear and carefully monitor its progress. We all excelled at school in nature studies.

Padgate School had a large cultivated garden with an apiary, for the students to learn the skills involved in bee keeping. We learned how to distinguish between the queen bee, the drones and the worker bees. We watched them as they swarmed and learned how to catch the swarm and collect the honey. We also learned about how different pollens affect the taste and how honey was so much more beneficial to you than sugar to sweeten foods. We used to wear a protective hat and gloves when working with the bees, but didn't bother with wearing the full suit.

I can remember one day I had been asked to give a talk to one of the younger classes. I had removed a honeycomb frame from the hive in order to point out the different cell sizes. The vast majority of the cells contain larvae that will hatch into the next generation of worker bees and are all of a uniform size, but the drone cells tend to protrude as their larvae are a bit larger. A queen bee larvae cell is significantly bigger and looks a bit like a peanut protruding from the honeycomb.

In order for the children to have a better view, I tilted the honeycomb frame on one side and to my utter dismay the wooden frame slipped off the metal clip I was holding and clattered to the floor. The startled bees were understandably angered and frightened by this and were determined to protect their hive. Fortunately, my head, face and hands were covered, but I was only wearing my school uniform shorts so my poor legs took the brunt of the bees' anger. The headmaster reprimanded me for getting too complacent and then sent me over to his house for his wife to pull out all the stings from my legs. He was concerned for my well-being, but also annoyed and saddened as many bees died as a result of my accident.

Fortunately, no one else got stung as the class observing my demonstration had been sitting in the safety of a specially prepared structure covered by a net. I remember being very proud of this, as a few months earlier my headmaster had called me and another boy into his office for a chat. He suggested that rather than continue with our woodwork class, where we made lots of fairly useless items, he would prefer to commission us to make an apiary observation room where a class could sit, observe and learn about bees without fear of being stung. He authorised us to purchase our own materials from selected local traders on his account and to design and construct the observation hide ourselves. We were thrilled to be entrusted with this task and once it was complete were extremely proud of our structure, particularly when it was put to the test in moments such as this.

Apart from our normal lessons we were also taught about personal hygiene and how necessary it was to clean our teeth using salt on a small toothbrush. I can remember the first time I used toothpaste was when our headmaster gave his permission for an agent to come into school to talk to us about the benefits of using their toothpaste instead of salt. We were all given a free sample to take home. My mother was very impressed with this new paste so bought us all a tin of Gibbs toothpaste for Christmas.

Christmas was always my favourite time of year. I loved sitting with my brother, sister and Hilda making presents for our family. We also made paper chain decorations that we would hang in our parlour. I can remember waking up on Christmas mornings to find my stocking at the end of my bed. It was always filled with chocolates, biscuits, fruit, nuts and paper hats, but most important of all was the silver sixpence that was always concealed in the toe. This sixpence always made me feel so independent, it was money that I could spend whenever and on whatever I wanted. However, I was never wasteful with money and it was only ever spent after a great deal of thought. Sixpence went a long way and could buy a significant number of things. We rarely took such a large sum of money as a sixpence in our shop. The most common coins in our cash drawer were farthings (which were a quarter of a penny) half penny bits and pennies. A packet of ten Woodbine cigarettes cost two pence.

Silver coins were actually made of silver so a silver sixpence was actually six pence worth of silver. A silver shilling was worth twelve pence, a silver florin (often called a two-bob bit), was worth two shillings; a silver half crown was worth two shillings and sixpence and a silver crown was worth five shillings. Very few people paid us with silver coins and it was always noteworthy whenever we had a crown or half crown in our cash drawer, so you can imagine our excitement at receiving a silver sixpence every Christmas.

We rarely saw any paper money in the shop, but my mother would order some items wholesale to supply other vendors. For instance, she supplied the local cinema with cigarettes and sweets and they often paid her for the bulk order with bank notes, such as a ten-shilling or twenty-shilling note.

No one we knew had a Christmas tree; the first one I saw was in a newspaper article my sister showed me. My mother explained that it was a tradition that Prince Albert, (Queen Victoria's husband), had brought into this country years before and that many wealthy households now had a tree in their homes at Christmas. It seemed like such a strange idea, but it did look beautiful. My most memorable Christmas present was a miniature fully working steam engine. My father and I set it up on the dining room table and set it going. Seconds later it ignited, not only setting fire to itself, but also the tablecloth and our dining table! Many buckets of water later the fire was finally put out, but our dining table was beyond repair. My mother threw what remained of the toy, the table and the tablecloth out into the back garden and that was the end of that present. That year Christmas dinner had to be eaten in the kitchen. It didn't matter though, our Christmases were always times of good food, games and laughter.

My mother was a very intelligent woman who had been privately educated. She taught us about economy and the importance of saving and putting money aside, how to be careful in outlay, not to be extravagant or wasteful and how important it was to learn from your past, but to always look forwards, never backwards and to keep your focus on your goals. Extraordinarily for this period in our history, my mother was always the main wage earner in our family and a very good businesswoman. She encouraged us to be helpful whenever we could, to always be polite, honest, loyal, reliable and trustworthy. Little did I realise at the time how much I would appreciate her tuition and advice much later in my life and always remember the feeling of warmth and security in our home. Security is such a simple word but it's incredible how much it means to a child and is the foundation on which adulthood is built.

CHAPTER 4

HOBBIES AND SPORTS

It was during this period of my schooldays that I took up boxing. The boxing club was situated above a public house in Warrington. Professional boxers, amateur boxers, wrestlers and gymnasts all trained in this club. It was in the boxing club that I was first given the nickname Curly as I had tight curls in my hair. The name also identified me from another much older boxer who was also called John.

I will always be grateful for the very good advice given to me by my trainer, a retired boxer called Jack, an amazing man who became a mentor to me. All these years on and I still remember him clearly, particularly his eyes; he just had so much wisdom in them and he could read people and their motives so well. He taught me a great deal, not just about coping in the boxing ring, but in the arena of life as well. He would often proudly quote the Latin phrase *"mens sana in corpore sana"* meaning "a sound mind in a healthy body". Smoking was a national pastime and greatly encouraged, but he was adamant that smoking was bad for your health and insisted that anyone wishing to train with him must not smoke. He called alcohol, "the devil's water" and insisted that trainee boxers should not drink any alcohol until they were old enough, and then only in small quantities. He said that we must keep fit and make sure that our minds and bodies were operating at their peak at all times. One of his favourite phrases always stayed with me: "Never underestimate an opponent and be ready for action at all times." This focus of making sure your body and mind were always working at their optimum was extremely good advice and I'm sure helped me to face all the challenges of warfare later on in my life.

Whilst I was boxing, my older sister went dancing at Warrington Parr Hall, which was close to the gymnasium where I trained. She was only allowed to attend these events if I escorted her and collected her on my way home from my boxing training. I often had to hang around waiting for her so it was during this period that my sister Cissie taught me how to dance. I took to dancing very easily and really enjoyed it.

One evening I was dancing with my sister when an "Excuse me Foxtrot" dance came on. A short time into the dance there was a tap on my sister's shoulder and a girl said "excuse me" and asked to dance with me. The young girl and I had just started to dance when my sister, who was furious at losing her dance partner, deliberately tripped the girl up sending her tumbling across the dance floor. I pulled the poor embarrassed girl back onto her feet, apologised for my sister's actions and we carried on dancing, but the glares from my sister warded off any future flirtations.

Other than boxing and dancing our other hobby was training our dogs. During the late 1930s we owned four greyhounds. One of our relatives owned a golf course where my dad and I played golf. My father insisted that he had purchased the dogs in order to chase and catch the rabbits that caused a lot of damage to the fairways. However, this was really just the way my father justified owning the dogs to my mother, the main reason my father kept greyhounds was to race them. My father had actually purchased some very good racing dogs and they won several local races.

One of the major racing events went on for a whole week and all the greyhounds had to board at the track kennels for the duration of the event. We knew our dog would do really well as it already had an exceptional record in Ireland before my father bought it. The main championship was held on the last day of the event and our dog qualified with ease. My father planned a family outing for us all to go and watch. The night before the event we were just getting ready to go to bed when there was a scratching at our front door. My father opened the door to be greeted by a rather tired and sore-footed greyhound that had not only managed to escape, but more remarkably had managed to find its way home. We were all delighted to see the dog home, but my father was furious as he knew the dog hadn't escaped of his own accord and had been deliberately set free to prevent him running and winning the race.

There were too many incidents like this in the world of greyhound racing, so in the end my father decided to sell all the greyhounds. I can remember us children all sobbing as we just wanted to keep them as pets, but my mother had decided that we would soon be moving from our bungalow in the country, to a newly built house in the centre of Padgate `and there would be no space for greyhounds or for Oner. The pony got sold with the bungalow and the dogs were sold and crated off to their new owner, much to our dismay.

Our new home, was a brand new, three-bedroom, semi-detached house, the second house on the right as you entered Delery Drive. The house was equipped with all the latest modern conveniences and had electricity in all the rooms. The bathroom was upstairs with a fully plumbed-in bath and toilet, with mains drains. It was also close to a regular bus service to Warrington and surrounding areas which really pleased our mother as she had found life in the country a bit too isolated. It was also useful for Cis and I when we travelled into Warrington for my boxing training and our dancing. Our mother always gave us the return bus fare, but we mainly opted to walk home and spend our bus money on buying a pennyworth of chips, first from one fish and chip shop and then when we'd finished those from another chippy that we would pass on the route home. They came wrapped in a cone made from newspaper, so the black print on our hands always betrayed how we had spent our money!

Delery Drive was very close to the perimeter fence of the RAF station at Padgate. A lot of my boxing opponents were RAF staff members from the base. It was interesting talking to them as it gave me an insight into RAF life, which did intrigue me, but at the time I wanted to be a professional boxer when I grew up. Most of my matches at this time took place at Warrington Parr Hall.

Our new house was much closer to our school, with footpaths all the way, but we did miss the lovely countryside route we used to take from our old house. I received an amazing education at Padgate Church of England School. Mr Rice, the headmaster, realised that I was capable of more than just a standard education, so went to the trouble of getting me extra books that took me to the next level in science, maths and algebra. I will always be extremely grateful for the amount of time and trouble he went to in order to give me the best education he could provide. Apart from academics Mr Rice also taught us to look up to and respect our parents and elders and to care for pupils younger than ourselves. This headmaster also had a cane in his office, but I'm not aware that he ever used it. I loved school and always worked hard, but even so I had a mischievous side. One day the boy sitting next to me was daydreaming, so when the teacher asked him to spell the word potato, he had completely missed what the teacher had said, so I whispered behind him and he repeated "S.P.U.D". The teacher did well to hide her amusement, but made me write out the word potato one hundred times.

I really enjoyed dramatic art classes in school, and took part in a number of concerts and plays, sometimes taking an acting role or on other occasions playing my Lorenzo piano accordion. In one of these plays I was given the part of a police sergeant, little knowing that I would become a police officer later on in my life. Sadly, I didn't keep up playing the piano accordion and soon lost my skill with this instrument, I had too many other things to occupy my time.

My school joined the rest of the nation in celebrating the crowning of King Edward VIII on 20th January 1936. Sadly, he only remained King until 11th December as he abdicated when the government refused to give him permission to marry an American, Wallace Simpson because she was a divorcee. After his abdication he married Wallace, was given the title the Duke of Windsor and went to live in France. This event completely rocked the nation as we were all taught to put your duty to your family, your community and your country above your own ambitions and desires, so it was extremely shocking that our King should choose his desire to marry Wallace over his duty to Great Britain.

After his abdication the crown passed to his younger brother Prince George. Therefore, a year later, on 12th May 1937, we had a second coronation to celebrate when King George VI and his wife Queen Elizabeth were crowned. The coronation was a time for Great Britain to celebrate her empire with dignitaries from all over the globe invited to attend. I can recall having to study the many territories that were associated with or governed by the British Empire. It was incredible to consider that such a small island as Great Britain had so much influence around the world. I remember listening to the radio news broadcasts and reading in the newspapers about the various dignitaries and honoured guests arriving on commercial airlines, in aircraft such as the popular Douglas Dakota DC3. It was exciting to see and so exotic. Most people flew into Croydon Airport, but I remember reading in the paper that the small airport at Heathrow might also be developed to take airliners. It was difficult to imagine that there was enough demand for air travel to require two airports near London. Passenger flights were also available from Liverpool and there were plans to use Manchester Airport for commercial flights as well. Flying was a luxury that could only be afforded by the very rich and famous and something the rest of us could only read about in newspapers.

Mr Rice our headmaster encouraged us to join the RAF Cadets as he explained that if we were lucky and conscientious, we might get offered a flight in one of the RAF's training aircraft a DE Havilland Tiger Moth biplane.

I loved learning all about aeroplanes in school and how the Wright brothers had flown the first controlled, sustained flight, in a powered, heavier than air aircraft, called the Wright Flyer in 1903. It was amazing to learn how quickly aircraft had developed from the Wright Flyer to seeing guests flying in for the coronation in the DC3 and other commercial airliners.

I can remember being astounded one day to see a huge object appear in the sky above Warrington. It turned out to be the German built Hindenburg LZ129 Zeppelin. It made quite a spectacle and I was determined to find out as much as I could about it. I found a newspaper article that said that this zeppelin was the largest aircraft ever manufactured, being 804ft (245 metres) in length (nearly as long as the Titanic) and 134ft (41 metres) wide. It was powered by four reversible 890KW Daimler-Benz diesel engines, which provided a maximum speed of 85mph, but it was raised aloft like a balloon, by hydrogen gas. I was stunned watching it cruise overhead - it was awesome and seemed surreal.

The newspaper article reported that as the airship passed over Yorkshire, one of the passengers, a German priest, dropped a parcel from the zeppelin, which when opened contained a small silver crucifix and a wreath of carnations, with instructions to the finder to please place the contents on the grave of his brother Lieutenant Franz Schulte. His brother had died in Skipton Prisoner of War Camp during World War 1 and was buried in Morton Cemetery, Keighley, in Yorkshire. The package was found by a couple of boy scouts who carried out these wishes.

I can remember that my parents did not share my fascination with the zeppelin, as they were not at all impressed to see a German airship flying boldly in British skies. During World War 1 German zeppelins flew over London and holiday resorts such as King's Lynn and Great Yarmouth, throwing bombs overboard and killing lots of people and injuring many more including young children. The Hindenburg had been built to carry passengers and freight on transatlantic flights to the USA, but nonetheless my parents and many others, saw it as a threat of German power and did not welcome it flying over their homes. Not long after this, on 6th May 1937, the Hindenburg crashed in flames, killing 32 of its 36 passengers and all 22 members of the crew. One member of the ground crew also died. It was believed that the accident might have been sabotage.

Mr Rice our headmaster did a project with us all about the Hindenburg disaster and the history of flight. When teaching us, we noticed that he had a habit of touching his neck and chin with his hands, as though in pain, and we heard that this was due to his having been gassed while serving in the trenches during World War 1. Chlorine gas was used a lot by the Germans against our troops, killing and maiming large numbers. Many who survived had their lungs permanently damaged like our wonderful Mr Rice.

Chlorine gas is now used to protect rather than to maim, used in minute quantities in water to purify it and in swimming pools to stop the spread of waterborne disease.

In 1938, a few weeks before I left school at the age of fourteen, Mr Rice visited my parents to discuss my future. He recommended that I should become an engineering apprentice. He explained that he had a friend who was in senior management at a large engineering company that dealt with all forms of machinery including locomotives. It was a wonderful opportunity and because of my glowing school report my interview turned out to be a formality. I was thrilled to be offered the apprenticeship that paid the sum of five shillings per week and enabled me to attend educational classes studying engineering, physics, geometry and science. The firm was situated in another town some miles away so my parents bought me a bicycle. I had to travel through all types of weather to reach my work, but it never bothered me, I was just so delighted to have found such excellent and exciting employment and to be learning such an incredible trade.

CHAPTER 5

VETERANS

Shortly after my fourteenth birthday I remember us all sitting around the radio listening to a broadcast by our Prime Minister, Neville Chamberlain. It was 30th September 1938 and he had just arrived back in Great Britain by aeroplane, after a meeting with Adolph Hitler in Berlin. I remember us all being much relieved to hear his reassuring words that his talks with the German leader had gone well. Mr Chamberlain stated in his broadcast:

"I believe it is peace in our time."

That evening my parents had a number of close friends and family over for drinks and light refreshments. My brother and sister had gone to see a film in Warrington, so, as I had no one of my own age to talk to, I decided to sit discretely in a corner of the room with a book. I soon became deeply absorbed in my reading, until the conversation turned to discussing Neville Chamberlain's speech on the radio earlier that day. This caught my interest and I started listening to the conversation.

The guests were all discussing the horrific thought of the possibility of a second world war. They were still all recovering from the stark realities of the World War 1 and no one wanted to go through that again. Some of my parent's guests, as well as my father, had been foot soldiers in the trenches. My father's sister had married Ernie Miller and he was in the cavalry. Uncle Ernie was a quiet, dignified man, who had clearly been greatly affected by his experiences in the war. My father had definitely been affected too, but he reacted by living for today and generally left my mother to deal with all the important issues in the family.

The men discussed how easy it had been for underage boys to join up to fight; my uncle said the military recruitment officers must have been aware, but if the youngsters said they were old enough, no one bothered to ask for proof. Going to fight for your country was glamorised and boys were encouraged to sign up. The men said how powerful the poster of Lord Kitchener pointing a finger with the slogan "Your Country Needs You" had been. They recalled how newspaper articles led the reader to believe that the war wouldn't last long and that Great Britain could expect an easy victory. Young lads liked the idea of returning home as victorious soldiers. There was also the promise of a free uniform, free lodgings, the payment of a few shillings a week and above all the opportunity to visit foreign countries, which would otherwise be an impossible dream for most of them.

Once enlisted the glamour talk stopped and the reality kicked in. The men discussed how shocked they were by the speed with which they were declared ready for combat and shipped overseas; they barely knew how to use their equipment. Once in France they were straight into the true horrors of war, witnessing their friends being slaughtered or suffering severe injuries themselves. Others were just terrified and suffering from shell shock. They talked about the absolute horror of having to use dead bodies to decrease the depth of the mud in order to be able to wade through the trenches during combat. The trenches were often knee deep after heavy rain. They struggled to get any sleep because of the images in their heads and the rats running over them, gnawing at their boots. To add to this, there was no chance of washing and most soldiers ended up with lice. They talked about how they had been given cigarettes and advised to take up smoking as it "calms your nerves."

They lived in dread of the sound of the whistle commanding them to "go over the top". This required them to scramble out of the slippery ditches and advance towards enemy lines, cutting through barbed wire, while under heavy machine gun and rifle fire from the enemy. They talked about how in the panic of the situation they would find themselves treading on dead and dying comrades. It was absolute and horrific carnage. It was obvious listening to these men that they had no respect for the officers stationed in complete safety, miles from the action, handing out the orders to advance and spectating over the whole scene like children with toy soldiers.

My uncle Ernie recalled how virtually every soldier ignored the rule that they were not allowed to waste valuable ammunition to put a dying horse out of its misery. I was touched listening to this old cavalry man, a hardened campaign soldier, who had watched so many friends die in combat, speak so tenderly about fallen horses. Over eight million horses died during World War 1. Virtually every farm and leisure horse had been commandeered by the armed services and shipped over to the front line. The death rate was so high and the demand so great that extra horses had to be shipped in from other countries. At one point over 1,000 horses a day were being shipped from the USA, others were shipped in from Spain, Portugal, Argentina, India and even as far away as New Zealand. In 1914 the British Army only owned 80 motorised vehicles so depended almost entirely on horses to transport everything including food, water, ammunition, weapons, troops, the injured and the dead. Horses were also used directly in combat by the cavalry. Uncle Ernie said how distressing it had been to see dying and dead horses strewn everywhere. He had joined the cavalry because he loved horses, but spent most of the time seeing them abused, injured and dying. He was a quiet man who rarely showed any emotion, but you could hear the anger and sadness in his voice. One thing that upset him greatly was that after the war most of the surviving horses were sent to market, as it was too costly to ship them back to Great Britain and many were slaughtered for meat. He felt very bitter about that as like most who have been through combat will tell you, life is precious and a surviving warhorse did not deserve that end.

Years later I read the following poem called *A Soldier's Kiss* by Henry Chappell which reminded me of my uncle Ernie and his passion for the warhorses that had served with him.

A Soldier's Kiss by Henry Chappell

Only a dying horse! Pull off the gear,
And slip the needless bit from frothing jaws,
Drag it aside there, leaving the road way clear,
The battery thunders on with scarce a pause.
Prone by the shell-swept highway there it lies
With quivering limbs, as fast the life-tide fails,
Dark films are closing o'er the faithful eyes
That mutely plead for aid where none avails.
Onward the battery rolls, but one there speeds
Heedlessly of comrades voice or bursting shell.
Back to the wounded friend who lonely bleeds
Beside the stony highway where he fell.
Only a dying horse! he swiftly kneels,
Lifts the limp head and hears the shivering sigh
Kisses his friend, while down his cheek there steals
Sweet pity's tear, "Goodbye old man, Goodbye".
No honours wait him, badge or star,

Though scarce could war a kindlier deed unfold;
He bears within his breast, more precious far
Beyond the gifts of kings, a heart of gold.

As I sat in my parents' front room quietly eavesdropping, I can remember having to strain to hear as they confided in one another. It was truly upsetting listening to those men talking in hushed tones about the torture of watching a comrade screaming in pain and pleading to be shot. One of them had witnessed one of his comrades being shot by a firing squad for failing to obey the order to go over the top. The threat of the firing squad was used to keep discipline, something else that hadn't been mentioned to underage teenage boys signing up.

The Shot at Dawn campaign was set up years later. Its primary aim was to grant pardons for those soldiers who had been shot by a firing squad after being found guilty of desertion, cowardice, or refusing to carry out orders. The campaign highlighted that the court martial in each case was very brief and execution followed soon afterwards. Those condemned to death usually had their sentences confirmed by Field Marshal Sir Douglas Haig on the evening following their court-martial. A chaplain was dispatched to spend the night in the cell with the condemned man and execution took place the following dawn.

When the time came, the offender was tied to a stake; a medical officer placed a piece of white cloth over the man's heart and a priest prayed for him. Then the firing line, usually made up of six soldiers, was given orders to shoot. One round was routinely blank so that no one in the firing squad could be sure if he had fired the fatal shot. Immediately after the shooting, the medical officer would examine the man. If he was still alive, the officer in charge would finish him off with a revolver.

A Shot at Dawn campaigner, John Hipkin argued that:

"So many of those who were executed were just boys, they made no allowance for that. No allowance was made for the soldier's mental state nor how long they had been fighting on the front. They and their families were let down. The whole issue was, and still is, a disgrace".

Hipkin recalled:

"One of the saddest cases was that of Herbert Burden, who had lied about his age in order to join the army and fight for his country, at only 16 years old. Ten months later, he was court-martialled for fleeing after seeing his friends massacred at the battlefield of Bellwarde Ridge. He was court-martialled and shot at dawn by the firing squad and yet he was still officially too young to have signed up."

I had learned all about World War 1 in school - Padgate, Church of England - and how many old pupils had died fighting for our country. Reading factual accounts was totally different to hearing it first hand from those who had truly experienced the horror of the front line. In school we learned to recite the poem *In Flanders Fields* written by a soldier, John McCrae. Major John McCrae was a Canadian military doctor and artillery commander who was asked to conduct the burial service for a good friend, Lieutenant Alexis Helmer. Helmer was killed on 2nd May 1915 in the gun positions near Ypres in Belgium. It is believed that later that evening, after the burial, John wrote his now famous poem.

Tragically, McRae died from pneumonia just before the end of the war in 1918, but his poem means he will never be forgotten, as it is the reason that poppies are now used to commemorate all those who have died defending their country.

In Flanders Fields by John McRae

In Flanders fields the poppies blow
Between the crosses, row on row,
That mark our place; and in the sky
The larks, still bravely singing, fly
Scarce heard amid the guns below.
We are the Dead. Short days ago
We lived, felt dawn, saw sunset glow,
Loved and were loved, and now we lie
In Flanders fields.
Take up our quarrel with the foe:
To you from failing hands we throw
The torch; be yours to hold it high.
If ye break faith with us who die
We shall not sleep, though poppies grow
In Flanders fields.

SCHOOL DAYS

1938

Myself, Cis and Bert on May Day in our
Sunday best outside our shop in Winwick
Street, Warrington.

My school leaving photo – aged 14.
Taken at Padgate Cof E School.
(Original image: hand-tinted B&W photo)

Acting the role of a policeman in a school play.
This must have been a formative moment, as I would go on to join the Police Service after
World War 2 and my service in the RAF!

Me with my boxing trophies.

My father, Herbert Meller, during the time of his service in the Great War.

My uncle Ernie, on his cavalry horse during the Great War.

CHAPTER 6

THE OUTBREAK OF WAR

On 3rd September 1939, I was at work operating a lathe and deep in thought. My fifteenth birthday was in a couple of weeks, so I was planning what I wanted to do with my day. The radio was on in the background in our workshop, when we all heard the radio announcement made by our Prime Minister, Neville Chamberlain, in which he explained:

> "This morning the British Ambassador in Berlin handed the German Government a final note stating that, unless we heard from them by 11 o'clock that they were prepared at once to withdraw their troops from Poland, a state of war would exist between us. I have to tell you now that no such undertaking has been received, and that consequently this country is at war

with Germany". He ended his speech stating: "Now may God bless you all. May He defend the right. It is the evil things that we shall be fighting against - brute force, bad faith, injustice, oppression and persecution - and against them I am certain that the right will prevail."

Everyone in the workshop looked concerned and we were all talking about it. I couldn't wait to finish work so that I could get home to discuss this with my family.

When I arrived home, I could hear my parents already discussing it. My dad mentioned how Lloyd George, (who was our Prime Minster at the end of World War 1), had warned that this would happen. A strip of land known as the Polish Corridor had been taken from Germany as a penalty at the end of the war and they were now claiming it back off Poland. Lloyd George had stated his concerns that this would eventually fuel another war and predicted that it would happen within a twenty-year time period. How right he had been!

The 3rd of September 1939 became known as "the day the balloon went up", for as soon as war was declared barrage balloons and searchlights were immediately brought into action in London, coastal ports and all other major towns. Barrage balloons were large tethered balloons that were used to defend the area below them from aircraft attack. The numerous steel cables tethering the balloons made it impossible for aircraft to fly beneath them, thereby protecting the object below from being bombed. In some areas a steel cable net was suspended between several balloons. These nets were a good defence against dive bombers and did offer a moderate amount of protection to the area below them from the unpiloted V1 Buzz bombs, which came later in the war.

Apart from the barrage balloons, it became most apparent that we were completely unprepared for war. Our current Prime Minister, Neville Chamberlain and his MPs were greatly berated for declaring war on Germany without first preparing us for battle. It was clear to everyone that our nation was extremely vulnerable.

Thankfully, France had also declared war on Germany, which helped our morale, as France was so much better prepared than us, having a huge army, an impressive air force and a superb fleet of ships.

There was much criticism of our government during this period, as whilst most men were being conscripted into the services, some politicians were still heading off on their holidays. However, the main criticism was aimed at Neville Chamberlain and how naïve he had been. It was of great concern to learn that Joachim von Ribbentrop, a Nazi politician and diplomat and close advisor to Adolph Hitler, had been the pre-war German Ambassador in London. When Neville Chamberlain became Prime Minister and moved into Number 10 Downing Street, Ribbentrop even rented Neville Chamberlain's London home in Eaton Place from him.

During his time in Eaton Place, Ribbentrop maintained

a close friendship with Chamberlain and entertained many prominent people. It was now feared that he had been able to obtain a lot of confidential information for Hitler and the Nazi Party. Ribbentrop clearly used his close friendship with Chamberlain to convince our Prime Minister that the Nazis offered no threat to Great Britain. If Ribbentrop had managed to fool Chamberlain, then Hitler did an even better job. In their meeting in Munich during September 1938 Hitler managed to convince Chamberlain that Great Britain had nothing to fear and Chamberlain returned declaring that: "We regard the agreement signed last night ... as symbolic of the desire of our two peoples never to go to war with one another again." Yet exactly one year later we were at war, but without any forward planning or preparation.

It was Hitler's skills as a powerful orator that had enabled him to rise from begging on the streets as a young artist, to becoming a corporal in the German army and then later into politics becoming the Fuhrer and Dictator of Germany. Hitler also knew how powerful media was in controlling a nation's thoughts and beliefs, so when he came to power, he immediately took control of the national newspapers and radio stations. The news headlines proclaimed, to the German people, how their new strong leader had brought full employment and prosperity to their nation, which had previously been on the poverty line. At this period in Germany, there were areas in many of the major cities known as the "Jewish quarter". In these areas it was virtually impossible to get work unless you were Jewish, and the Jewish work ethic and business acumen meant that they controlled quite a lot of the commerce in the cities. Many people were angered by this monopoly. The media (under Nazi control) praised Hitler for getting "the Jewish problem under control", but no mention was made as to the horrific manner in which this was being implemented.

In Great Britain our media was full of horrendous stories relayed by our intelligence personnel as well as from Jewish people who had managed to escape from Germany. Hitler's hatred of the Jewish people was extreme and the stories from survivors and those who escaped were dreadful to read. The Nazis would round up Jewish people and send them to concentration camps where many were murdered or used as slave labour and their property confiscated. It was state organised pillage. Many thousands of Jewish prisoners were used as human guinea pigs to trial drugs. Mass graves were dug to bury those who were murdered.

Whilst these atrocities were going on in Europe, Great Britain was still in shock. Other than the balloons going up, the only other sign that we were at war were the information leaflets sent out to every household. I can remember when ours arrived we all sat down as a family to read all the information and procedures.

The leaflet explained all about the Blackout that had to be observed by everyone. No lights were to be seen from any building during the hours of darkness. The gas streetlights were all to be left unlit at night. Thin curtains had to be lined with a heavy material, or the windows had to be painted black. Strips of brown paper tape were to be pasted on to the inside of windows to reduce the danger of injury from shattered glass. All vehicle headlights had to be shaded so that they could barely be seen and the kerbs were to be painted white so drivers could see them in the dark. Wardens were to be introduced to patrol all streets to make sure that the Blackout was enforced.

A National Registration Identity Card was to be introduced which you had to have on you at all times and have readily available for inspection by a police officer or warden if requested. These cards remained in force until six years after the war, but were only issued to civilians and not to members of the armed forces.

Ration books were to be introduced to control the distribution of food and other premium items. The first item to be rationed was petrol. The 29th September 1939 became known as National Registration Day when every householder had to fill in a form giving details of all the people living in that household. Each person was then issued with a ration book. At first there was still plenty of food around, but as the war progressed rationing became vital in order to ensure that everyone, rich and poor managed to get sufficient food to eat. The first ration coupons were dated 15th September 1939. They came in three colours; pink for babies, blue for children from four to 14 years old and beige for everyone over the age of 14. There were government restrictions on food prices to prevent the cost of food rising and the poor not being able to afford to eat. We had separate ration books, one for petrol, one for clothing and one for food. The only food items that were not rationed were bread, potatoes, vegetables, fruit and fish.

Turn-ups on the bottom of men's trousers were the fashion at the time, but due to the shortage of material, they were banned. Most of us felt this was a great improvement, as turn up trousers always gathered dust and dirt. The rationing of clothing included the slogan: "Make Do & Mend" and did not end until 15th March 1949. A lot of techniques were brought in to make food go further; we were told not to peel potatoes and to eat peas still in their pods. Some people went too far in trying to optimise food and I can remember a warning on the radio telling listeners to be careful about eating sausages as some butchers were adding sawdust to the meat to make it go further. Food rationing carried on long after the war, until 4th July 1954.

Air raid sirens were installed throughout the country. They had different sounds, one for an air raid and another for the all clear. There was a ban put on ringing church bells as they were only allowed to be rung as a warning of invading troops parachuting in or landing on our beaches. The government leaflet gave the following directive that in the event of hearing church bells civilians were advised to stay indoors, hide all maps, immobilise all bicycles and motor vehicles and to avoid engaging into any conversation with the enemy.

Anderson shelters were erected in gardens for people to use in the event of an air raid. They were steel shelters with curved roofs and were distributed to most households considered to be vulnerable and which had sufficient space to put them. Morrison shelters (steel cage tables) were provided for protection in homes considered to be vulnerable to air raid attacks that didn't have sufficient space to erect an Anderson shelter.

The London Underground stations were to be used as sleeping quarters. Thousands of Londoners marked out permanent areas for their portable beds and personal belongings. They were not allowed to use them before 6pm except during an air raid. Public baths, schools, warehouses and similar buildings were all designated for emergency use. Large pits were dug in graveyards, in case a mass grave was urgently required and papier mache coffins were constructed for areas where casualties were expected to be high.

Alternative accommodation was found to evacuate the royal family which consisted of King George VI, Queen Elizabeth, Princess Elizabeth aged 13 and Princess Margaret aged nine, but the royal family refused to leave. When asked to evacuate Queen Elizabeth famously stated:

"The children won't go without me. I won't leave the King and the King will never leave."

The Palace lost most of its staff to the armed services and many of the rooms were covered in dustsheets, their doors locked and no longer used. Many of the Palace windows were shattered by bomb blasts and were boarded up. Buckingham

Palace and its grounds were hit sixteen times by aerial bombs. The fact that the royal family refused to be intimidated by this and were at the centre of the Blitz suffering alongside the nation helped tremendously with morale.

Even though the royal princesses stayed in London, approximately three million children, living in our most vulnerable cities, were evacuated to live with families in the country. Each child was given a label to wear on which their parents wrote their name and their home address. Their parents were told to pack each child a gas mask, change of underclothes, night clothes, plimsolls, spare socks, toothbrush, comb, towel, soap, facecloth, handkerchiefs and a warm coat. The directive stated that all belongings must fit into one small bag or a pillowcase. They had to say goodbye to their parents without knowing where they were going to end up. They were accompanied by a few adults, who acted as guardians and who would ensure that they were rehomed.

With so many child evacuees to be rehomed some were even sent abroad to live in the USA, Canada, Australia, and New Zealand. Tragically some children never made it to their destination as their ships were sunk by German U-boats. Thankfully, the vast majority of children found sanctuary with wonderful caring families in the countryside where they could grow up with little fear of air raids and the horror of war. Sadly though, some ended up in homes where they were used as a form of slave labour doing menial tasks for little or no reward. The children and their new guardians were instructed to write to their parents, using the home address on their label to inform them where they were now living.

Children were not the only ones evacuated. Hundreds of poisonous reptiles and dangerous animals were either evacuated to more rural zoos or destroyed. Pet food production was greatly restricted and as a result many people had their pets put down. People were also encouraged to slaughter any unessential horses. This provided an additional source of meat and meant that these animals were not eating valuable forage required to feed farm animals. Horsemeat that was not fit for human consumption was made available for pet food but was dyed green to identify it.

The leaflet explained that all males between the ages of 18 and 41 years would be conscripted into the armed forces, so I still had three years to wait until I was 18 years old. Many women volunteered to sign up as well. Recruitment centres were set up around the country. Any men not conscripted were encouraged to offer their services as local defence volunteers. This body, officially called the Home Guard, soon earned the nickname "Dad's army". These men were given armbands so that in the event of an invasion, it was hoped that they would be treated as soldiers, whereas an armed civilian would be shot. Everyone was encouraged to attend Air Raid Precaution (ARP) classes to learn how to put out fires, first aid and how best to protect yourselves and loved ones during an air raid. I went along with my dad to one of these courses held in our village hall.

Iron garden railings were to be pulled out and melted down

to be used to make munitions and people were encouraged to donate any metal objects not completely required to be recycled and made into aircraft. There was a big campaign asking for "pots and pans for planes".

To optimise food production a survey was conducted of all British farms and each farm was placed in a category depending upon its level of productivity. Farmers were given lectures on how to increase output and were given many incentives to do so. Those who were incapable or unwilling to make these necessary changes were forcibly evicted from their own land and their farm was given to others deemed to be more capable. Maximised productivity from every scrap of land was vital to keep the nation fed. People were instructed to pull out flower borders and replace them with vegetable patches. Those with large enough gardens kept chickens and many with large gardens, built pens and kept at least one pig or a goat, whilst others kept rabbits as a good source of protein. Whilst Great Britain was busy gardening, the Germans were busy sinking our merchant ships to prevent them delivering valuable resources to the country.

CHAPTER 7

CHURCHILL TAKES CHARGE

O n 9th September 1939, a few days after war was declared, a British Expeditionary Force of four infantry divisions sailed across the English Channel to France to assess the situation, particularly along the Franco-Belgium border. By March 1940 Britain had 316,000 soldiers stationed in France. They sent back information stating that the trench warfare of the World War 1 was no match for the modern warfare techniques we would be facing against the Nazis. Despite the fact that the combined force of the British and French soldiers outnumbered the Nazi army, the German armed forces were a modern, well equipped, disciplined and extremely professional military force, both on the ground and in the air.

If Neville Chamberlain was still in any doubt about the devious intent of the Nazi party it was soon confirmed when Hitler invaded Belgium, Luxembourg, Norway, Denmark and the Netherlands. Men from the invaded countries were rounded up as forced labour to help in the German war effort.

It was election time in Great Britain, but the country had neither the time nor the resources to waste on party politics, so it was decided that it would be best to form a coalition government. On 10th May 1940 Winston Churchill was appointed as our new coalition Prime Minister. Winston Churchill was the son of Lord and Lady Randolph Churchill whose residence was Blenheim Palace in Oxfordshire. Winston Churchill was a fabulous orator and his speeches were the inspiration the nation needed to pull together. Churchill had considerable experience as an army officer, serving abroad in Cuba, India, Egypt and the Sudan, which was extremely advantageous to a Prime Minister leading his country into battle.

On 13th May Churchill made his first speech as our new Prime Minister, in the House of Commons in Westminster. He stated:

> *"On Friday evening last I received His Majesty's commission to form a new Administration. To form an Administration of this scale and complexity is a serious undertaking in itself, but it must be remembered that we are in the preliminary stage of one of the greatest*

battles in history … I hope that any of my friends and colleagues, or former colleagues, who are affected by the political reconstruction, will make allowance, all allowance, for any lack of ceremony with which it has been necessary to act. I would say to the House, as I said to those who have joined this government: I have nothing to offer but blood, toil, tears and sweat. We have before us an ordeal of the most grievous kind. We have before us many, many long months of struggle and of suffering. You ask, what is our policy? I can say: It is to wage war, by sea, land and air, with all our might and with all the strength that God can give us; to wage war against a monstrous tyranny, never surpassed in the dark, lamentable catalogue of human crime. That is our policy. You ask, what is our aim? I can answer in one word: It is victory, victory at all costs, victory in spite of all terror, victory, however long and hard the road may be; for without victory, there is no survival. Let that be realised; no survival for the British Empire, no survival for all that the British Empire has stood for, no survival for the urge and impulse of the ages, that mankind will move forward towards its goal. But I take up my task with buoyancy and hope. I feel sure that our cause will not be suffered to fail among men. At this time I feel entitled to claim the aid of all, and I say, come then, let us go forward together with our united strength."

It was most apparent from the outset that with Churchill there would be no deals, no armistice, no accords with Hitler. It had to be total victory or total defeat. The government under Churchill introduced a new law called the Emergency Powers Act that gave it almost unlimited authority over every person and all property, including banks, wages, profits and conditions of work. It meant everything in Great Britain was now under state control.

Churchill welcomed to Great Britain all displaced government personnel in exile from the Nazis, as well as all foreign service personnel and civilians who had escaped from their homeland before or after German occupation. The majority of immigrant service personnel immediately volunteered and joined our military services.

A common fear of being ruled by Hitler made the British public pull together with one spirit and one mind to protect our freedom. The war effort and "doing your bit" was one of the main topics of conversation and I couldn't wait to be old enough to become part of the fighting force.

Whilst Great Britain was selecting a Prime Minister, Hitler was busy invading Europe. The whole of Europe was now living in fear of the Nazi war machine and most people felt that it was only a matter of time before Hitler successfully invaded Great Britain. We had been happily enjoying a short period of peace after World War 1 and had been duped into believing that the Nazis were no threat. In the meantime, Hitler had been fine-tuning an army fit to conquer a massive empire. By comparison, the only plan of defence Great Britain appeared to have at the outbreak of war, was a few barrage balloons, some instruction leaflets and some land mines with rolls of barbed wire set out along the beaches. Anti-aircraft guns were speedily being erected at strategic points around the country, but the crews to operate them still needed to be trained. Each gun crew consisted of between 10 to 12 people. Many women helped operate these defence guns, including Churchill's own daughter, Mary Soames, who served at a gun site in London's Hyde Park. Women were not allowed to serve in combat, so could not officially arm or fire the guns, but they took on vital roles necessary for the operation of the guns. Women worked as spotters, using binoculars to find enemy planes, range-finders who calculated the distance a gun shell would have to travel to hit the target and predictors who worked out the length of the fuse necessary to make sure the shell exploded at the right height.

The government was so convinced that invasion was likely that special invasion committees were set up and secret hideouts constructed. Selected people were appointed to wage guerrilla warfare in the event of invasion by the Germans. Methods were put in place for putting undercover agents into strategic places in Europe to glean intelligence. Underground secret intelligence offices were set up in different parts of the country. The secrets you manage to keep and the lies you manage to convince the enemy of can be hugely important to the outcome of war. Great Britain was particularly clever at the art of espionage.

A D-notice was introduced with the co-operation of the media, meaning that certain information was not allowed to be broadcast or to appear in print. It is obviously not advantageous for your enemy to know that their attack has been successful, so the D-notice enabled the British Government to put a positive spin on broadcasts and news reports. British radio stations were given false information so that German agents would pass this on to their superiors. Pre-agreed phrases were used in news articles as codes to send information and instructions to our secret agents listening to the radio abroad. All Germans living in Great Britain were interned, even though they may have been pro-British. Southern Ireland declared that they wished to remain a neutral zone during the war and did not wish to declare war on Germany. Therefore, people were warned to be careful about sharing information or offering strategic jobs to people from the Republic of Ireland as there was a threat that Nazi activists could enter Great Britain that way.

Churchill's government introduced Double British Summer Time (DBST) in order to put us on the same time zone as Germany. The aim was to prevent any errors occurring by time zone differences between the two countries. In the autumn Great Britain normally puts its clocks back one hour, but in 1940 the clocks were kept at British Summer Time (BST). In the spring Great Britain normally puts its clocks forward one hour, which it did in 1941, meaning that we were now two hours ahead of GMT, (GMT+1 in the winter, and GMT+2 in the summer). I can remember what a difference DBST made to me as I rode my bicycle to and from work. The government noted that DBST meant fewer people had to travel in the dark, which meant fewer accidents and less work for the hospitals treating civilians. Statistics proved that there was less pollution, due to burning less fuel, particularly for domestic use and street lighting. DBST was a huge success, so to this day I still can't understand why we didn't continue with it after the war.

The government passed a law making it compulsory for all women between 18 and 60 years of age, to offer their services to work as part of the war effort. Over seven million women took on jobs; no other country utilised its civilians more effectively to keep its nation running smoothly. I cannot explain the impact this had. I had grown up in a world where few women worked outside their homes and very few received any education after leaving school at the standard school leaving age of 14 years. Women normally had a staid and very predictable existence, expecting little more from life than the satisfaction of having served their husbands and raised their children, but now due to the conscription of men, there was an acute shortage of workforce in all forms of employment. Women were now suddenly legally obliged to find care for their children and join the workforce. They were employed in all vital war work, working in factories, making munitions, engineering and maintaining vehicles and aircraft. Land Army girls kept the farms running, women became police officers, ambulance crews and fire fighters. Female pilots became members of the Air Transport Auxiliary, which ferried aircraft around the country from the factories where they were built and transported them in from overseas. The Women's Timber Corps, commonly known as Lumber Jills, kept wood supplies going. The government employed many young women, as decoders, encoders, cryptographers and code breakers, stationed at various secret locations. Since the outbreak of war, women were suddenly being appreciated for their many talents and skills and were receiving the respect they deserved. It gave them a new sense of freedom and independence. These women became the backbone of our country keeping everything running. One thing was very clear, both they and future generations would no longer be happy to simply return to the kitchen sink ever again.

CHAPTER 8

THE BATTLE OF BRITAIN

I t is unbelievable how close Hitler came to invading Great Britain. At the time that Churchill took up office as our new Prime Minister, the Nazi army were in the process of invading the Netherlands and our army was in the midst of a huge battle, alongside our allies defending France from Nazi invasion. Four days after Churchill came to power the Germans had burst through the French / Belgium border into the Ardennes region and then turned towards the English Channel. The Allied army was almost defeated and the German Panzer Division with their well-equipped tanks were only 15 miles away from the remaining Allied soldiers. Then, suddenly, the Germans halted their advance. To this day, no one is completely sure why they stopped their onslaught. For three days they waited, which gave the Allies the chance to regroup and await evacuation from the beaches of Dunkirk.

Our military ships were unable to reach the shore as the sea was too shallow, so a fleet of shallow draft boats was required. The British Ministry of Shipping was tasked with finding a fleet of shallow hull boats. Once suitable vessels were found, they were commandeered by the government, with or without the owner's knowledge. All manner of boats were used, from tugboats, cabin cruisers, cockleboats, barges, fishing boats and trawlers. The most important factors were that they had a shallow draft and that they were seaworthy. Once they were fully fuelled, they were then taken to the fishing town of Ramsgate in South East England, where they all rendezvoused before setting sail as a fleet for Dunkirk. The majority were manned by naval officers, but other vessels were crewed by experienced civilian volunteers, such as fishermen and a few of the private boat owners volunteered for the mission too. The evacuation took nine days to complete, finishing on 4th June 1940 and was code-named Operation Dynamo. The evacuation was a huge success incredibly saving the lives of over three hundred thousand Allied French and British soldiers.

Immediately after the rescue mission Churchill said in an address to the nation:

> *"We shall go on to the end. We shall defend our island whatever the cost may be. We shall fight on the landing grounds; we shall fight in the fields and in the streets. We shall fight in the hills we shall never surrender."*

After our troops had been evacuated, the French were left on their own, still under invasion. They had already sustained huge causalities, so the French politicians decided that it would be easier to collaborate with the Nazis rather than continue to fight. On 22nd June 1940 the French ordered their troops to cease fire. They surrendered without first giving notification to the Allies, they didn't even allow time to hand over their fleet of ships or any equipment to the British, they just handed everything over to Hitler, in order to try to appease him.

As soon as Churchill was notified that France had surrendered, he ordered the impressive fleet of French naval ships to be destroyed to prevent Hitler using these resources against us. He knew that this would tragically result in the loss of a number of French naval crew lives; a decision that must have been hard to make.

After France surrendered Hitler divided France into two zones. The northern zone was run by the Germans and the southern zone was run by a Vichy puppet government. The Germans ordered all French men to register giving their dates of birth and those aged between 19 and 32 were sent to work in German factories or to assist the German military forces.

The French managed to set up a secret army gathering vital intelligence to aid the Allies and cause as much hindrance to the Nazis as they were able. It is estimated that there were over 100,000 men and women actively involved in this movement which was known as the French Resistance. Their work played a significant role in the war effort.

The whole of Europe and many other countries around the world were now living in fear of the Nazi war machine. Many decided it was best to form an alliance with Hitler in an attempt to appease him. Soviet Russia had already signed a non-aggressive pact with Hitler in August 1939 and now other countries followed suit. Some countries declared themselves to be neutral including Spain, Portugal, Sweden, Switzerland, the Vatican City, Liechtenstein, Afghanistan, Turkey, Monaco, Yemen, Saudi Arabia, Andorra and San Marino. Denmark, Belgium, Norway, Luxembourg and the Netherlands all declared themselves neutral, but were still all invaded by Germany.

The countries that joined Great Britain and our Commonwealth by declaring war on Germany were Australia, New Zealand, Canada, Brazil, Newfoundland and South Africa. Young men from all these countries and all over the Commonwealth served as our Allies.

The USA remained neutral, with their congress simply stating that, they did not want to get involved. However, the US President, Franklin Roosevelt did everything he could to help the British war effort. He started a lease / lend agreement covering the cost of all materials and food shipped over to Great Britain and he sent a fleet of US Navy ships to protect their merchant fleet delivering these supplies.

With Germany now controlling most of Europe, Great Britain stood alone. The German army seemed unbeatable to us, they were so professional, experienced and well-armed. Morale is hugely important in a crisis and the power of rousing songs and of Winston Churchill's inspirational speeches cannot be underestimated. The wartime music, songs and entertainment provided by legends such as Glenn Miller, Vera Lynn, Gracie Fields, Joe. E. Brown, Tommy Handley, George Formby and Bud Flanagan all helped to keep our nation fighting on.

An all-time great was Vera Lynn's:

> *There'll be blue birds over the white cliffs of Dover, tomorrow, just you wait and see.*
>
> *There'll be love and laughter and peace ever after, tomorrow when the world is free.*
>
> *The shepherd will tend his sheep, the valley will bloom again and Jimmy will go to sleep, in his own little room again.*
>
> *There'll be blue birds over the white cliffs of Dover tomorrow just you wait and see.*

At 16 years of age, I was still too young to directly join the war effort, but I was very proud to be a member of the Royal Air Force Cadets. One of my best experiences with the cadets was being taken as a passenger in a Lysander aircraft. It was an unbelievable experience; unlike anything I had ever known. The whole concept of being able to take to the air was incredible. I bored everyone silly with my excitement of that experience.

I had always been keenly interested in aviation and my recent flight had furthered my enthusiasm, so when I heard that a new airfield had been opened at Burtonwood, and that they were recruiting engineers I decided to enquire. I went for an interview at the new Burtonwood Repair Depot, I was accepted for the job and started the following week.

My first sight of Burtonwood airfield was one of astonishment and disbelief. It had been a few years since I last visited this area as a child, playing in the meadows with my brother and sister, it was here that we had been caught in a thunder storm and had been taken in by a kind lady to shelter and dry off. I couldn't believe the changes. Where there had been countryside and open fields, now these acres were covered in hangers, warehouses, workshops, offices and dispersal areas. There were various types of aircraft, long runways and plenty of activity. To my eyes at the time, this was no desecration of the countryside, but instead it was sheer magic.

I soon discovered that many of the craftsmen working at Burtonwood were refugees who had escaped from France, Belgium and Poland, all of whom could speak good English. During break times I would sit and listen with great interest, particularly to how they had managed to escape and the atrocities they had endured or witnessed. It was exciting to meet people from different countries, to hear their stories and learn little bits of their language which they enjoyed teaching me.

At the Repair Depot I worked on many types of aircraft, mainly on the electrics, I often worked a twenty-four-hour shift, with only short breaks in between for naps. We were only paid a normal working week wage, as under the government's new Emergency Powers Act, no one was paid any overtime; everyone was expected to do the extra hours for free as part of the war effort. Instead of overtime payments we were given a Promissory Note, which was a written guarantee from the government, promising to pay you a contribution to your over time wage at some point in the future; if and when they were able. It was some time after the war ended that I received a small sum of money from the government, as a back payment for all those hours of work, but none of us did it for the pay.

I remember being told by one of my supervisors at Burtonwood that I didn't need to worry anymore about being called up to join the services when I turned 18 years old. He explained that I would be exempt from fighting now, as my employment at Burtonwood was classified as a reserved occupation, meaning that my skills at the Depot were vital to the war effort. Despite this I knew that nothing would stop me from signing up. Having spent many happy moments watching the aircraft take-off and land at Burtonwood I even fancied that I might volunteer as aircrew.

It was around this time that I also heard a lot of talk about a young man, whose relatives lived locally, who had registered as a conscientious objector, on both moral and religious grounds and had refused to take any part in the war effort at all. He had been sentenced to imprisonment as a result. It caused quite a stir as most people who did not wish to fight usually managed to get around it by taking on a reserved occupation, or offering to join the Royal Army Medical Corps. I did understand their views as I certainly didn't want to kill anyone either, but having heard the atrocities happening in Europe first hand, from the refugees I was working alongside, I didn't want to witness that happening on British soil and I was prepared to do whatever was required to prevent that, or at least die trying.

After our defeat at Dunkirk, Great Britain held her breath, as everyone thought we were about to be invaded. This is why the rallying speech made by Winston Churchill, on 18th June 1940, is possibly one of his most important:

> *"What General Weygand called the Battle of France is over. I expect that the Battle of Britain is about to begin ... Hitler knows that he will have to break us in this island or lose the war. If we can stand up to him, all Europe may be free and the life of the world may move forward into broad, sunlit uplands. But if we fail, then the whole world, including the United States, including all that we have known and cared for, will sink into the abyss of a new Dark Age made more sinister, and perhaps more protracted, by the lights of perverted science.*
>
> *Let us therefore brace ourselves to our duties, and so bear ourselves that, if the British Empire and its Commonwealth last for a thousand years, men will still say, 'This was their finest hour'."*

Churchill's speeches were a major factor in keeping the nation together and focused. They were always encouraging and sympathetic, but also strong fighting words that made us all push on when at times we felt defeated.

On 10th July 1940 Hitler started a major aerial attack on Britain. The sustained battle for aerial supremacy continued from July to October 1940 and became known as the Battle of Britain. By September 1940 Hitler commenced high intensity bombing raids of Great Britain's major cities, but primarily of London. The period between September 1940 and May 1941 became known as the Blitz. On one occasion London was bombed on 57 consecutive nights. The word Blitz originates from the German word *blitzkrieg* meaning lightning war. It must have been terrifying and over 180,000 Londoners spent night after night in underground shelters, and in the underground railway stations, but tragically thousands of civilian deaths were still recorded. Londoners listened to the continual drone of German bombers overhead, our anti-aircraft guns and to the screaming of the sirens sending out their warnings. They listened to the terrifying sound of high explosives and incendiary bombs as they hurtled down, wreaking indiscriminate death and destruction.

Many major cities where hit in a similar manner, Coventry, was so heavily bombed that the whole of the city centre was almost eradicated.

All the emergency and voluntary services were kept busy day and night, with large numbers of their members getting very little sleep. Dogs were trained to help trace people buried among the rubble. Electricity, gas and water supplies often had to be cut off due to damaged lines and so it was common to have to queue with buckets at the nearest standpipe and many people had to use candles and torches for light at night. Food was increasingly scarce and often it was difficult to even get the meagre rationed amount.

Where such opportunities arrive, there will always be a small element of people who try to use these situations to their own advantage. There were reports in the newspapers about thieves caught looting from bombed out shop fronts. The Home Guard were given orders to shoot on sight anyone seen looting, as a deterrent to others. These incidents were thankfully a rarity as most people were all pulling together to save their country and care for one another.

Thousands of people were homeless, but still Great Britain kept running. Londoners took the greatest onslaught but they stayed resourceful, resilient and defiant. In May 1941 Germany decided that this strategy wasn't working and even though air raids continued the main Blitz was over.

I was only 16 years old during this period and Padgate wasn't a major target, so other than hearing about it from radio broadcasts and newspapers I was lucky not to be directly involved. Government D-notice restrictions played down the impact of the Blitz, so it wasn't until a few years later when I was stationed in London that I truly realised the devastation that had been caused and what those living there must have endured.

On 27th September 1940, as Great Britain was still coping with the Blitz, the war escalated further when Japan and Italy signed a Tripartite Pact of alliance with Nazi Germany to form what became known as the Axis group. At this point the only two major fighting forces world-wide not currently involved in this war were Soviet Russia and the USA.

Soviet Russia's leader Stalin and Hitler had signed a non-aggressive pact on 23rd August 1939, yet despite this, on 22nd June 1941 German troops invaded Russia. This was to become the largest invasion in the history of warfare, as during the course of the attack three million German troops, 600,000 motor vehicles and 700,000 horses were deployed. Germany conquered a lot of land in the Ukraine and seemed set to invade much further into Soviet Russia, but then the Russian winter settled in and the war soon became a battle of attrition against the elements. As soon as German troops invaded Soviet Russia, Stalin immediately pledged to join forces with Great Britain and her Allies in our fight against Hitler.

At the same time that Hitler was trying to conquer the whole of Europe and attack Soviet Russia, Japan was also trying to conquer Asia, and also had its eye on eastern Russia. The Japanese must have been feeling very confident with their conquest of Dutch East Asia, Malaya and China, but felt that forming the Axis alliance with Hitler and Italy's Mussolini could only increase their strength.

In 1941, Hideki Tojo, became the new Prime Minister of Japan. Tojo suspected that the USA would possibly send war ships out to Asia to defend some of these territories. To prevent USA intervention Tojo decided to destroy as many US Naval war ships as possible in one hit, by bombing them whilst still in port at one of the US Navy's largest bases, Pearl Harbour, in Hawaii.

On 7th December 1941 Japan attacked Pearl Harbour. The act that was intended to ward off US intervention caused the opposite effect, as now the full might of the USA was focused with full force and absolute rage on Japan and Hitler. The USA first declared war on Japan on the 8th December and then pledged her allegiance to Great Britain and her allies, by declaring war against Nazi Germany on 11th December 1941. There is little doubt that without the combined might of the USA and Soviet Russian armed forces, Great Britain and her other allies could not have held the might of the Nazis and the Japanese aggression at bay for much longer.

Now that the USA had joined the war in Europe, she needed a base nearer the front line and so several RAF bases around Great Britain were transferred over to the United States Air Force (USAAF). The RAF station at Burtonwood was one of them. Burtonwood soon became one the largest US bases in Great Britain and home to the US Eighth, Ninth, Twelfth and Fifteenth Air Force units.

I was still working at Burtonwood when the news came in that it would soon be transferred to the USAAF, but by the time the transfer went ahead in June 1942, I had already been offered a premium apprenticeship engineering position, with a family run firm in Warrington. My old headmaster Mr Rice had once again helped me by providing a letter of reference. This job offered a normal working week with no over time required and paid the most I had earned up to this point, at ten shillings per week, which was an excellent wage for a seventeen-year-old lad. The working hours at my new job were ideal as they enabled me to keep up with my boxing training as well as attend an evening class to further my education. This job was not classed as a reserved occupation, which suited me as I had always intended to sign up as soon as I was eighteen.

Even though I no longer worked there, I would still sometimes ride my bike past Burtonwood. It was astounding how things had changed in only two years.

Ready for my RAF interview.

CHAPTER 9

TIME TO SIGN UP

During September 1942, as soon as I turned 18 years of age, I applied to the RAF to volunteer as aircrew. A few weeks later I was called for a selection interview at RAF Padgate. The selection board consisted of five RAF officers and the process included a formal interview, a stringent medical, as well as several academic and physical tests. At the end of the selection day I was delighted to hear that I had passed all the necessary requirements, to a sufficiently high enough standard, to be selected for PNB recruitment (Pilot Navigator or Bomb Aimer). I went home full of excited anticipation to await my official letter from the Air Ministry. When the letter arrived a few days later, I was really disappointed to read that although I had passed the selection for PNB, there were currently no places available on these courses. The letter explained that many of the places on the current courses had been filled by foreign applicants who had volunteered for these posts. The Air Ministry explained that I could either wait for a place to become available, (but they anticipated a considerable delay), or if I wanted to enlist immediately, I could still become an aircrew member by joining as a wireless operator or rear gunner as there were immediate spaces available on those courses.

That evening we sat down as a family to discuss my options. I can remember my mother starting the conversation by saying how uplifted she was to hear that thousands of young men from other countries were volunteering to join our fight against Hitler. Reflecting on this, I had to agree that it was incredible that so many young men were prepared to leave the safety of their own country to enter a war zone and volunteer as part of the Allied force. Many of these brave men gave up their lives defending Great Britain and democracy. It was humbling to think of this and made me all the more determined to volunteer immediately and take the first aircrew course available.

The next day I wrote my letter to the Air Ministry accepting to be trained as an Aircrew Wireless Operator, both my parents were of the opinion that I had made the correct decision. A school friend of mine, who attended the same selection interview as me, opted to wait for a pilot training course to become available. He had a couple of years to wait until he was finally called up and sent out to Canada for training. He had literally just finished his course and returned home with his wings as the war ended, so I definitely made the right decision.

The day I left home to join the RAF my mother presented me with a silver chain on which was fastened a silver St Christopher. She made me promise to wear it whenever I was flying. I had been given a train pass by the Air Ministry and had to make my own way by train from Padgate down to Stockley Hall in London.

The journey itself was quite daunting for me as I had never travelled very far from Warrington before. I was astonished taking in all the sights and sounds of London and I was shocked at the devastation caused by the intense bombing by German aircraft during the Blitz, and could see why it was often referred to as the second Great Fire of London. On my arrival at Stockley Hall I was taken into the administration department and immediately given a personal crew number, a set of digits I will never forget, 2209216. I had to provide this number in order to collect my wages which were a couple of shillings per week. This was a big pay drop from my premium apprentice wage. I was issued with my uniform and a large kit bag in which to keep all my personal belongings, and on which I had to inscribe my name and number for identification purposes. I was also given a piece of white cloth to fix to my cap to denote that I was trainee aircrew.

I could not believe the apartment I was billeted to in Stockley Hall; I had never seen anything like it before in my life. I was given a luxury apartment with an en-suite bathroom and shower cubicle. It was a complete marvel to me to be able to enjoy my own private shower. A number of these luxury apartments had all been commandeered by the Air Ministry to house its trainee aircrew.

Once I had unpacked, I was instructed to join the other trainee aircrew on parade in the adjacent courtyard. We were then marched along the streets of London until we reached London Zoo. This was my first visit to London so I was in wonder of all the sights as we marched. We were taken to a restaurant at the zoo and told that this was to be our regular dining place for all our meals whilst we were billeted there. We were then taken around the zoo, which was now permanently closed to the public and shown the layout with its remaining incumbents. All the dangerous animals had already been either destroyed or evacuated to more remote zoos, but it was our duty to try to protect and detain any animals that escaped in the event of an air raid damaging their cages. Myself and another trainee were detailed for night patrol of the zoo for a couple of nights. We were given access to the zoo's restaurant as a base for the evening.

On my first day at Stockley Hall I remember feeling really uncomfortable in my uniform trousers as they had not held their crease and I just didn't feel very smart. By the following morning I had picked up a good trick to maintain my uniform trousers. Just before bed I would slightly dampen the trousers along the crease and then place them carefully between my under blanket and my mattress. The next day they looked freshly creased and tidy and I felt so much better.

My previous Air Training Corps experience helped me a great deal in these early weeks. I remember being really proud when, after only a week, I was selected to march the troops to and from each meal at the zoo. My moment of pride was short lived when I realised I only had a vague idea of how to find the zoo, as up until now I had simply been happily marching along behind the other recruits in my own world of thoughts. Thankfully, one of the lads was a Londoner and knew the area well, so I made sure I put him in the lead and we set off with me supposedly leading the way.

The training was strict but fair. There was plenty of physical training and lots of drill work. They also took us for swimming lessons to Hendon Baths where I obtained my life saving certificate and badge. We also took part in several swimming contests against other service personnel from other areas. Our swimming instructor stressed how essential it was for aircrew to be able to swim, as it could save our lives if we had to bail out or crash land in the sea, which he warned had happened on a large number of occasions.

I really enjoyed all of our academic training; it was intensive but so interesting. We learnt about radio receivers, Morse code, transmitters, radar and aircraft recognition. I found it all so interesting and my young brain just soaked it all up. Amazingly, I can still remember certain items learned then, to this day. For instance, the first ever radio signal was transmitted over a distance of one mile in 1895 by an Italian scientist called

Guglielmo Marconi, when he was only 21 years old. There were numerous written and oral tests and I always did well.

Being stationed in London gave me the opportunity, along with a couple of the other recruits, to tour different parts of London. It was during our sight-seeing tours that we first saw for ourselves the terrible destruction of buildings by the Luftwaffe, which included well known buildings such as the House of Commons, Westminster Abbey, Westminster Hall, St Thomas' Hospital, St James's Palace and St Paul's Cathedral, all of which had been hit by bombs a number of times.

All the shop windows had to be boarded up, but it was still fascinating looking around all of the big department stores. It was whilst I was stationed in London that I saw my first television set, although it wasn't in use. They were only for sale in London, as before the war you could only watch television if you lived within a certain radius of Alexandra Place in North London, as that was the site of the only television mast in Great Britain. As soon as the war broke out, the British Broadcasting Corporation (BBC) had to stop all television transmissions and the aerial was used to jam German aircraft navigation equipment instead. It was not until after the war, in December 1949 that a second television aerial was installed in Sutton Coldfield which covered the Midlands, but still the remainder of Great Britain had no television coverage.

Whilst taking in the huge amount of damage inflicted upon London, I remember being properly aware for the first time of how important aerial supremacy was during this war and being pleased with my choice to join the Royal Air Force. Thomas Grey, Poet Laureate in 1757, almost two hundred years before the aerial warfare of World War 2 appears to have had incredible insight when he wrote:

"The day will come when thou shall lift thine eyes to watch a long-drawn battle of the skies, and aged peasants too amazed for words, stare at the flying fleets of wondrous birds. And England, so long mistress of the seas, where winds and waves confess her sovereignty. Her ancient triumphs yet on high she bears and reign the sovereign of the conquered air."

1942, the year I was enlisted as a volunteer aircrew member, was also the year that Sir Arthur Harris was appointed Commander in Chief of the Royal Air Force. On taking up this post Harris declared that:

> *"The Nazis entered this war under the rather childish delusion that they were going to bomb everyone else, and nobody was going to bomb them. At Rotterdam, London, Warsaw and half a hundred other places, they put their rather naive theory into operation. They sowed the wind, and now they are going to reap the whirlwind."*

Although the main Blitz was over, air raids over London and other major cities around the country continued sporadically throughout the rest of the war.

I was with two other cadets on one of our sightseeing tours, when we heard the screaming of the air raid sirens, but as we were already heading back in the direction of St John's Wood and didn't have too far left to go, we decided to ignore them and just hurry back to Stockley Hall instead. A few minutes later we heard the drone of aircraft engines overhead, above the clouds and heard the anti-aircraft guns shooting into the sky, so we rushed to the nearest underground station, which fortunately for us was nearby. As we entered the underground, we could hear the terrible sounds of war and commotion with bombs exploding nearby, but as we ventured deeper into the tube station, it was like entering a different world. Instead of seeing fear, pain and anger on the faces of the underground occupants, we found a community of friendship, trust and immense spirit.

There were beds and personal belongings everywhere and different family groups had their own marked out areas, where they returned every night and whenever the sirens went off during the day. Buckets were used for toilets, which were kept at the extreme end of the platform and emptied daily by railway staff.

Although it was packed, people still squeezed up to make room for us. One man played the piano accordion, which made me feel a little homesick for mine back at home, others joined in with mouth organs, and we all joined in singing our favourite wartime songs. It was an evening that I shall always remember, stuck in an underground station with strangers having an amazing sing-a-long, whilst bombs exploded over our heads. When the all clear signal was sounded a huge cheer went up, but we were enjoying the camaraderie so much that we stayed for some time afterwards. As we left, we could still hear those voices singing: "Land of Hope and Glory, mother of the free, how shall we extol thee, who are born of thee."

On leaving the shelter of our underground station we were soon hit by the sight of the destruction caused by this latest raid. It was shocking after the amazing morale-lifting environment of the underground station to suddenly be standing in the midst of this destruction. I will never forget seeing two elderly ladies who were almost hysterical, standing looking at a pile of rubble, presumably once their home. I felt devastated watching their anguish and feeling helpless to alleviate it for them. All of the emergency services were already there working very hard. The Women's Voluntary Service van pulled up beside the wreckage and its volunteers started handing out hot cups of tea and were just there to offer reassurance, comfort, guidance and advice to those who were now without homes and possessions. My last glimpse of the elderly ladies was of them being led away covered in a blanket and clutching a cup of hot tea.

We offered to stay and help, but the rescue services thanked us and told us that the emergency services could cope and that we would be better just concentrating on getting home safely. I remember getting into bed and feeling impatient to take up my post in Bomber Command and have a proper role to play in the war effort.

CHAPTER 10

RAF Bridlington

Stockley Hall was beautiful, but sadly we were only stationed there a short while before we were told to pack our kit bags ready to leave. The following morning several RAF fabric-covered lorries were waiting to transport us to our new base in Bridlington, Yorkshire, which was also known as Carnaby Airfield. I can still feel the mixture of excitement and trepidation I had as I clambered into the back of the lorry. During that bumpy uncomfortable journey, I was aware that this was suddenly the transition from anticipation to the reality of what I had enlisted to do.

Our base at Bridlington was indeed a rude awakening after the luxurious, centrally heated, en-suite apartments that we had just left, and stood as a forerunner of what we could expect from then on. When I was based at Bridlington in 1943, it was still in the process of being developed as an airfield, had no runway or hangars and was just a large field with a scattering of Nissen huts. When the runway was eventually built, the base was moved a little further inland, but whilst we were stationed at RAF Bridlington it was merely a field full of Nissen huts right by the beach. Some of the huts were used as lecture rooms and others as dormitories. Our dormitory was equipped with a stove in the centre and a total of ten beds, five on either side. The beds at least were very comfortable, each equipped with woollen blankets and clean crisp sheets. The ablutions included an outdoor shower, which was a dramatic change from our Stockley Hall en-suite shower rooms. Fortunately, it was now June and the sun was shining, so we all soon settled in and began to enjoy the relaxed atmosphere and the companionship of being billeted together.

Bridlington also had another redeeming feature, which we only became aware of when we were told to present ourselves for Physical Training (PT) early the following morning. We had presumed that this would be conducted in the fields surrounding the huts, but much to our surprise, we were marched across the field, over the mound at the far end of the field and straight onto a glorious secluded white sandy beach. During the war it was almost impossible to find a beach that hadn't been sealed off by barbed wire fencing and covered in land mines, as a precaution against enemy landing craft. This beautiful beach was an exception and so it was not only used for our PT sessions, but also became a place to relax, unwind, sunbathe and swim during our free moments. This was a wonderful unexpected treat for teenage lads to have a beautiful beach for our leisure time and greatly boosted our morale. Sadly, our beach was soon to be fenced off with the standard defences and closed to the public, but we enjoyed it while we had the opportunity.

A few days into our stay at Bridlington, we were told that the Archbishop of York would be attending the church near our base. We were all encouraged to attend. The local congregation made us very welcome and the Archbishop offered us all a confirmation service. Many of us decided to be confirmed and were given our confirmation certificates and a Holy Communion Book that I still have. Inside the book was written; "John Henry Meller, confirmed at the RAF, Bridlington, Yorkshire, by the Archbishop of York 17/06/1943. J. F. Southworth, Chaplain RAFVR."

The lessons at Bridlington were much more relaxed than we'd been used to at Stockley Hall. Most of these lessons concentrated on the practical aspects of operating as new aircrew. We learned more about the specifics of the aircraft instruments we would be using, and there was more detailed instruction on aircraft recognition; including British, US and in particular German aircraft. We also learned to recognise German navy ships. We were told that poor aircraft recognition had meant that Allied aircraft had been mistakenly shot down with tragic loss of life.

We learnt the phonetic alphabet "Alpha, Bravo, Charlie" etc as well as how to pronounce numbers clearly over a crackly radio to prevent confusion. For instance, naught was "zero", one was "wun", three was "thuh-ree" four was "fo-wer" and nine was "niner".

Radio communication also used abbreviated terms such as "Mayday" meaning "we are in peril", "Oscar Mike" meaning "we are on mission", "Lima Charlie" meaning "I've heard your message loud and clear" and "Roger" meaning "I have received your message and understood it". The word "Snipers" was the code word used for enemy fighters. The dial of the clock was used to give position reports, particularly of enemy aircraft, to other crew members, for instance "snipers in your 4 o'clock".

We were taught the necessity of maintaining radio contact at all times both when training and during operations. We were taught how essential it was to be observant when airborne, not only looking for enemy aircraft, but also for our own aircraft, especially when closing in on a target on bombing raids. We were also told to look out for flocks of birds in flight as some migrating birds fly at high altitude.

If we ditched in the sea or had to make a forced landing, it was my responsibility to take the Very pistol with me on evacuating the aircraft. When fired the Very pistol distress flare could be seen for miles. The Very pistol could also be used as a weapon if directed at someone, so had to be handled with absolute care.

We were taught the location of the on-board tube of

morphine with a syringe and how to administer it in an emergency. We learned how to inject this directly into a vein, keeping the needle straight at all times.

We were instructed on how to use our oxygen masks, which had to be worn whenever we were above 10,000 feet. Each crew member had his own plug-in point for oxygen, but there were a few other plug-ins around the aircraft in case you needed to move to a different location.

We were warned about G-force; it could happen suddenly if the pilot had to put the aircraft into a sudden steep turn or dive to avoid enemy fighter aircraft. I can remember our faces when our lecturer explained that abrupt manoeuvres by the pilot would give the same motion as going at speed over a hump in a car except that in an aircraft the effect was far greater and could cause you to momentarily black out. This still didn't prepare me for the first time I experienced it and seeing the weightlessness of everything around me. Anything that wasn't tied down would become airborne during those brief moments. It was a good way of retrieving lost items though! I can remember watching a previously lost pencil floating next to me during a high-G manoeuvre.

Our lectures mainly concentrated on teaching us how to decipher and send messages using Morse code and learning how to operate the R1155 receiver and the T1154 transmitter sets, which just used Morse code to communicate. The pilot could speak to air traffic control towers within a certain radius, but after that the only way for us to communicate was by the

Wireless Operator sending and receiving messages by Morse code. We were told of the importance of listening out on the R1155 receiver at all times, just in case an instruction came through for a change of target or if the operation had been altered or aborted for any reason. We used the T1154 to send Morse code messages. In order to be able to decipher these messages we had to be able to receive and transmit Morse code at a speed of at least eighteen words per minute. I was able to do twenty-four words per minute. It was an essential skill and one you had to be able to use when under pressure, with lots of other noises and distractions, in the freezing cold and when being bumped around in an aircraft in the dark. Morse code was a major stumbling block for a number of the young lads on my course, if you couldn't reach a minimum of eighteen words per minute in the exam you were taken off the Wireless Operator course and your skills transferred to another avenue of operation.

We were instructed on the use of Oboe navigation. The system consisted of a pair of two radio stations in different locations on the English coastline, one known as Cat and the other as Mouse. The aircraft was fitted with a transponder that could return the radio signals sent from Cat and Mouse. Cat controlled the aircraft distance and Mouse controlled the aircraft track, using a similar system to Morse code. A dot signal told the pilot that the aircraft hadn't yet reached its target, a normal length dash signal meant they were over the target and a long dash meant they'd gone too far. Cat and Mouse could only direct one aircraft at a time, so Mosquito crews were trained to use the Oboe system and then used as pathfinders. They would fly ahead of the large bomber formations and once overhead the target the operator at Mouse would instruct them to drop their high-resolution flares. The bomber formations would then drop their bombs directly over the flares.

Oboe was first used in an air raid attack on 21st December 1942. Prior to Oboe, only about 10% of the bombs dropped actually landed on the designated target. The introduction of Oboe greatly increased the rate at which the target was directly hit.

Gee-H was introduced later on and worked on similar principles to Oboe, but just in reverse. With Gee-H the ground stations became the transponders and the navigator in the aircraft became the controller. This meant that multiple aircraft could use the system at the same time, enabling the bomber aircraft to navigate accurately to overhead the target without the need for a pathfinder.

British intelligence had determined that German radar only used three frequency ranges, making them prone to jamming, so a system called Window was soon developed to jam the German radars. Window was just lengths of aluminium foil dangling from tiny parachutes which when dropped from an aircraft generated a cloud of false echoes on the German radar screens. Window was the invention of British scientist Joan Elizabeth Strothers from Swansea in Wales. At night the Germans used radar to find incoming bomber aircraft. Once they had located the aircraft position the searchlights were then positioned to find the aircraft in the night sky and then the anti-aircraft guns would commence their attack. With the radars rendered useless the searchlights could only roam the sky aimlessly.

Window was first used as part of the bombing raids on Hamburg. Twenty-four crews were briefed on how to drop the bundles of aluminised-paper strips; treated paper was used to minimise the weight and to maximise the time that the strips would remain in the air, thereby prolonging the effect. A crew member in each aircraft would release one little parachute of foil strips out through the flare chute every minute, using a stopwatch to time them. The results proved to be spectacular. The German radar displays were completely jammed by false echoes, enabling the huge formation of heavy bombers to fly straight over Hamburg virtually undetected. It was such a simple but very clever invention and it made a massive difference to our operational safety. In this lecture we were each given an example of Window to take away with us and I've still got my sample to this day.

Whilst at Bridlington, I can remember gazing out of our classroom window and taking in the view. I could hear the hum of bees, which took me back to my schooldays. I remember thinking, I would never have imagined in my school years, that in a few years' time I'd be sitting in a Nissen hut in the middle of a field in Yorkshire, near a stunning beach, learning all about war tactics.

Whilst the bees worked busily outside my window our lecturer was explaining all about government security agents: MI5, MI6 and the Secret Service. We were told that most of the recruits for these organisations were approached whilst still studying at University, in particular Cambridge University. We learned that the British counter-espionage organisations were second to none and this was having a huge impact upon the possible outcome of this war. I was astounded to hear of things such as The Official Secrets Act and that systems such as bugging were currently being used to defend our country.

We were told that Great Britain had an excellent intelligent secret decoding centre that was providing our government with invaluable information about the enemy's strategies.

Much later, after the war, I heard that this centre was based at The Mansion, Bletchley Park in Milton Keynes, a beautiful old Victorian estate, which became an incredibly successful intelligence operation centre and was a major factor in us winning the war. At Bletchley Hall women outnumbered men and they covered all forms of work from general administration through to those who operated the Colossus computer. The Colossus was used to decipher the German Lorenz coding machine that the German High Command used to disguise important war strategy messages sent by radio telephony throughout Europe. The names of all the secret agents who were part of Great Britain's wartime code breakers have been published and includes the grandmother and great aunt of Kate Middleton, the Duchess of Cambridge.

Another invaluable secret service was the Y-service, which consisted of a chain of wireless interceptors across the country. Thousands of people worked for this service, the majority of which were young women, all sworn to secrecy and handpicked for their skills, particularly their ability to translate German. The agents would sit monitoring radio frequencies until they heard German pilots speaking when they would write down every word they could decipher. The pilots used codes for map references and targets and the women soon learned to break these codes and pass on the information. The women working these frequencies would regularly hear the same German pilot voices and would be able to recognise the voice from previous sorties. Those working in Y-service saved thousands of lives by enabling an early warning signal to go out concerning imminent bombing attacks on cities as well as enabling Allied fighter aircraft to scramble and protect essential sites, machinery and the personnel who worked there. They were a hugely significant force in the battle to protect our country.

Winston Churchill referred to these secret agents as "the geese that laid the golden eggs and never cackled."

Our lectures helped to lift our morale on how the war effort was faring. With the USA and Soviet Russia now as our allies, it was clear that the odds were now improving in our favour.

CHAPTER 11

46%

All young men in Great Britain were drafted into the services, but no one was forced to become aircrew, you had to volunteer, due to the extreme dangers involved. As volunteers, we were allowed to opt out at any time and our skills used elsewhere towards the war effort. Up until this point in our studies, our skills were easily transferable to other occupations in the RAF, such as engineers or ground crew wireless operators. It was explained to us that due to the increased complexity of radio and electronic devices being used in bomber aircraft, our training course was now one of the longest training courses for trainee aircrew. Our lecturer stated that due to the length, complexity and cost of the training they didn't want trainees to go all the way through the course and then drop out of an aircrew position at the last minute. The lecturer therefore requested that we think long and hard about what we were volunteering to do and that if we had any doubts, we should opt out sooner rather than later.

We were then given a lecture which outlined the immense risk we were taking as aircrew. Many of the young men on our course were volunteers from overseas, who had signed up to fight for Great Britain and democracy. Our lecturer thanked all of us for volunteering and expressed his appreciation for the essential role we were committing to, as without people willing to take on these dangerous roles, we would stand no hope of winning the war. Our lecturer explained that the fatality rate for aircrew at that time was extremely high at 46%. He said that the back of a bomber was one of the most dangerous places to be in this war. If aircrew did survive air crashes sadly many of them experienced horrific burns.

Plastic surgery and the treatment of burns was still in its infancy at the time, but the medical profession had to step up and develop new methods to cope with the poor young aircrew damaged by fire. Thankfully, wherever there is a great need, a great person often steps forward, and in this instance, it was a pioneering surgeon, who specialised in skin grafting, called Archibald McIndoe from New Zealand. The aircrew he helped fondly called themselves the "Guinea Pig Club". All the nursing staff were made aware that the mental scars these young men carried were as important to treat as their physical scars. The importance of a positive, fun attitude with plenty of friendly banter was extremely important, but most of all they were taught to look these brave young men directly in the eye and never to shy away from them, no matter how bad their injury. Learning to adjust to a new, extremely compromised facial identity is a very difficult emotional transition, especially for those who are young and handsome. Attractive, bubbly female nurses who accepted and valued them in their new image were invaluable. McIndoe insisted that his patients continue to socialise, not only in hospital, but out in public too, as soon as they were physically fit enough to cope. The patients were unanimous when they said this surgeon literally gave them back their lives. This highly respected surgeon became Sir Archibald McIndoe when he was knighted and awarded the CBE in 1947, in recognition of his outstanding work.

We left our 46% death rate and disfiguring burns lecture more than a little shell-shocked. We knew the reasoning behind it, but it didn't help our morale much; we put it behind us and moved on. The outcome of World War 2 was dependent upon all of our military services conducting vital roles, but much of the outcome would depend upon aerial supremacy and we knew we were a small, but essential part of that fighting force.

During my leisure time at Bridlington I really enjoyed getting to know all the volunteers from various countries and talking on an intellectual level with well-educated, interesting men - both the lecturers and the students. Hot topics of conversation were issues such as "why did Hitler halt his troops in the battle of Dunkirk?" If he had kept up his advance, he could have completely wiped out our troops before they had time to evacuate. One of our instructors theorised that Hitler didn't really want a war with Great Britain, especially as our royal family were of German descent and that Hitler wanted Great Britain as an ally not an enemy. This was countered by an older volunteer who quite rightly asked, "then why did Hitler attack Great Britain with the Blitz". Another instructor stated that Hitler only started the Blitz as a result of us first bombing Berlin. It was a huge education listening to and engaging in these debates. We discussed the second battle of El Alamein in Egypt during the months of October and November 1942, where General Bernard Montgomery led his Eighth Army troops of British and Commonwealth forces to a tremendous victory over Germany's Nazi General Rommel, popularly known as the "Desert Fox". Little did I realise as we discussed these exotic places, that in a few years' time I would be based out in Egypt, flying over the area where this very important battle had taken place.

Another topic of conversation concerned the Treaty of Versailles signed in June 1919 at the end of World War 1. This stipulated that Germany was not allowed to construct any military aircraft for the next seven years, ending in 1926. The moment the ban was lifted, construction of a whole new generation of military aircraft commenced, so it was clear that Germany had spent the interim years working on aircraft designs. When Adolf Hitler came to power in 1933, he put tremendous resources towards creating a formidable air force and well-equipped military aircraft bases. Hitler named his impressive military fighting force the Luftwaffe. He first put this new combat force to the test in 1936, when it gained a lot of valuable combat experience supporting General Franco's nationalist forces during the Spanish Civil War.

We also discussed one of our more recent lectures, which had certainly shocked several of us. We all took our lectures very seriously, as it was pointed out that the government didn't have time to waste on our general education, so each lecture was deemed vital not only to the war effort, but also because the information might just save our lives. So, when we were given a lecture on one-night stands we were all a little shocked. I had never heard of such a thing before. In the community I had grown up in you knew that you must not have sex outside marriage and that if you did, both families and the whole of your community would be appalled and you would be obliged to marry the girl as soon as possible. No girl I had known would have consented to sex outside marriage. Yet here we were sitting in a Nissen hut in the middle of a field, in a coastal town in Yorkshire being warned about females who would try to have sex with you. We were told they could be of any age or background and that many now carried sexually transmitted diseases. We were told that because the war had moved a lot of people away from the guidance of their families and communities, one-night stands were now becoming a real problem and many service personnel were suffering from outbreaks of venereal disease (VD), syphilis and gonorrhoea, with their lives possibly in complete ruins. The government did not want to lose valuable aircrew, essential to the war effort, due to VD.

With the recent lectures on one-night stands and aircrew disfigured by horrific burns still uppermost in our minds, we were informed that it was time to leave the summer camp atmosphere of Bridlington behind us and move on to our advanced training. It was now September 1943 and I was just about to celebrate my nineteenth birthday. We were all granted one week's leave and given a free train ticket to help us travel from Yorkshire to our homes.

We were driven to the train station, but from there it was up to us to find our way home. It wasn't easy during the war as all the station names had been removed and nothing ran to schedule; trains just appeared as and when they were able.

I was lucky to catch a train travelling in my direction fairly quickly and soon settled back into my seat enjoying the smell, sound and rhythm of the steam train. It was very exciting to be on my way home and lovely to see how everyone appreciated those wearing a uniform.

I had to change trains, but soon realised that I'd missed the connecting train. I spoke to the conductor who said he had absolutely no idea when the next train would be available for that route so advised me to catch a bus instead. I was astounded to find that the bus driver flatly refused to take any money from me for my bus fare and gave me a brief salute. The bus got me as far as Warrington and then I walked the remaining couple of miles home to Padgate.

It was such a pleasure to see the shocked elation on my parents' faces when I walked in. Just being home with all its comforts and relaxation was such a treat. Being able to listen to the radio, or go to the theatre and cinema was such a freedom. My parents even treated me to a meal out at a restaurant to celebrate my visit home. It was lovely catching up with my brother and my sister too.

It was really interesting listening to the opinion of my parents and their friends on the progress of the war. At Bridlington we were locked in our own small world of study interspersed with some time on the beach and so had little time to listen to the radio or read the newspapers. I was surprised to learn about the "Bevan Boys"; a large number of conscripts, who, instead of being allowed to enlist in one of the armed services were presented with a pair of heavy safety boots, a hard hat and a lamp, and sent down the coal mines, shovelling coal to prevent a national energy crisis. The government had failed to list coal mining as a reserved occupation, vital to the war effort, so most of the experienced coal miners, whose families had mined those shafts for generations, had been enlisted into the armed forces, leaving the country desperately short of coal. The problem was that the Bevan Boys had no previous experience of mining and so production initially took a huge plummet. My parents were astounded by the government's lack of common sense that had allowed such a ridiculous situation to occur.

Another hot subject amongst family and friends was the

information that allegedly some criminals had been released from prison by the Secret Service as their "skills" were required to carry out certain tasks such as forgery and safe breaking.

It was wonderful to just have time to sit in a comfortable chair and catch up with reading the newspapers. Obviously, I knew that a lot of the news could not be fully relied upon for its accuracy, due to D-notices, but nonetheless I couldn't help but feel comforted by many of the articles. The news reports definitely left me with the impression that the war was at last changing in our favour, even if we still had a long way to go. Italy had just signed an unconditional surrender to the Allies. Mussolini had been overthrown and his Fascist government ousted, so over a period of a month Italy had switched sides and was now on our side. Many Italians had been disillusioned with Mussolini and his alliance with Hitler. This coupled with the Allies invading Sicily and bombing Rome, caused the King of Italy, Victor Emmanuel III to take action against Mussolini. In July 1943, Mussolini was arrested and the King appointed Marshall Pietro Badoglio as the new Italian Prime Minister. Badoglio immediately signed a pact with the Allies and declared war on Germany. On hearing this, Hitler instigated an invasion of Italy, captured a large area in the northern districts, rescued Mussolini and placed him in charge of it, but the majority of Italy continued under the rule of Marshall Badoglio and remained in alliance with the Allies.

I wasn't able to idly sit and read the newspapers for long though, as my parents soon put my time at home to good use.

I happened to mention that our lecturers had said it would be advantageous if we could learn at least a few simple phrases of German. They had suggested that this could greatly enhance our chances of escaping capture if we crash-landed or bailed out over Germany. My parents immediately engaged the services of a schoolteacher friend, who recommended that the quickest and easiest way to learn a few basics of another language was by learning some poems which included useful phrases such as the German lullaby:

"Guten Abend, gute Nacht, mit Rosen bedacht, mit Näglein besteckt, schlupf unter die Deck" (Good Evening, Good Night). That teacher's advice certainly worked because I can still remember those poems over seventy years later. I taught the poems to some of my fellow crew members and we made up German names for one another to use if we found ourselves stranded behind enemy lines. I chose the name Wolfgang. We would use some of the phrases as incidental speech and our German names when larking about, but it was good practice.

I would dearly have loved to remain at home for a few days more, but my journey had taken much longer than I had expected, so reluctantly I made the decision to leave a day earlier than I had previously planned, so that there would be no danger of being late back to base and risk missing my transfer.

Both my parents were there to say goodbye. My mother hugged me close saying hopefully the war would be over soon for everybody's sake. I knew she was desperately hoping that it would all end before my brother was enlisted as well. My mother reminded me of the St Christopher charm that I had promised to wear whenever I was flying. I stopped at the end of Delery Drive and had one last look back at my home before starting my journey back to base.

CHAPTER 12

ADVANCED TRAINING

The day the lorries came to transfer us down to Yatesbury, we all had to assemble outside our Nissen huts and it was only then that it became apparent just how many had dropped out of the course. You could opt out at any point right up until you received your commission, but from that point onwards failure to operate as a crew member would be deemed as Lack of Moral Fibre (LMF) or in the worst-case, desertion.

As I considered the attrition rate and our recent lectures on plastic surgery and our poor chances of survival, I did have to wonder at my sanity, but there had already been so many opportunities for me to legitimately opt out of front line operations and at each stage I had been determined to see this through. I wanted to be as big a part of the war effort as I possibly could – no matter what the end. If this war was going to be won then we all had to be prepared to stand and fight the best way that we could. I knew that there was no way that I would ever consider quitting. The fact that all the young men remaining on our course had faced the same demons and decided that this was a duty worth dying for made the bond between us even closer. We all shared the same resolve that we would rather stand, fight and die than be ruled by Hitler. As Churchill so rightly stated:

"We shall go on to the end. We shall defend our island whatever the cost may be … we shall never surrender."

There was a twenty-four hour armed guard on the gate at RAF Yatesbury to prevent unauthorised entry, with armed guards patrolling a fifteen-foot high fence around the perimeter. Yatesbury was a Gunnery, Wireless and Radar Training School which reminded me of RAF Padgate. As we drove through the gates, my eyes immediately alighted on the aircraft hangar that contained a Dominie and a Proctor aircraft and I was delighted to note that at long last we were to be based at an RAF station that actually had a functional runway.

Despite the improvement in facilities, we were still billeted in Nissen huts, but the beds as always were extremely comfortable and laundered regularly. The food in the mess, although mostly repetitive, was very good and a step up from the more basic provisions at Bridlington. There was a Navy Army and Air Force Institute (NAAFI) where we went to relax and I would often treat myself to a "Nelson Slice". I was told by one of the staff that this was a mixture of any spare bread, cakes or buns that remained at the end of the day and which were past their best. Instead of throwing them away they would turn them back into crumbs and use them as the main ingredient to make the Nelson Slice. As such the flavour of this dessert would vary a little each time. It was always delicious and a firm favourite at only two pence for a really large slice. This cake was named after the great English national hero Admiral Lord Nelson.

Our first day of training at Yatesbury was spent learning how to do a parachute jump. We were taken into a hanger in which a high-level platform had been constructed. We had to climb up a ladder onto the platform about twenty-foot high, grab a rope and jump down onto a couple of gym mats on the floor using the rope to slow our fall down. We had to practice keeping our feet together, our knees bent and to remember to roll on landing. We then had to pretend to quickly remove our parachute, roll it up and hide it somewhere out of sight. We learned how to pull the cord and how to fit a parachute, but we didn't actually ever do a jump from an aircraft.

Our most memorable day at Yatesbury was 12th November 1943 when we all had our first flight in a DH89 Dominie biplane aircraft, registration number X7381. We were all buzzing with excitement; most of the trainees had never been in an aircraft. This was my second flight as I'd been lucky enough to experience a flight a few years earlier when I was in the Air Cadets. It had virtually been a year since we joined up and we had been wearing the uniform, learning all about the workings of the aircraft and even how to parachute out of one, but up until now we'd hardly even seen an aircraft, let alone fly in one. Sadly, three trainees had to drop out of aircrew training as they became uncontrollably airsick virtually as soon as they left the ground. I was pleased to hear that they were all kept on at Yatesbury as their knowledge and skills were now to be put to good use as ground crew instead.

Thankfully, I didn't suffer from airsickness and flying absolutely thrilled me. I will never forget that flight - flying through clouds and seeing the world from a bird's eye view. I loved the vibration, the smells and the wonderful splutter and rumble of the de Havilland Gypsy engines. I was in my element.

There was an excitement I experienced that day that never left me. There was something about the cacophony of sound, motion and smell that made me feel almost at one with these wonderful bits of machinery. Floating above the Earth and looking down on the land and sea is a sensation I shall never forget. What a privilege it was to be aircrew. I logged eleven hours and forty-five minutes flying time whilst at Yatesbury and loved every minute of it.

I went back to the classroom with a renewed vigour. Lessons now became directly relevant to how we would shortly be operating. Our navigational course included how to take bearings from a loop aerial so as to pinpoint one's position. Just over a year later, I ended up using this technique to navigate our route back home from Germany when all our other navigation equipment had been destroyed by fire.

There were a large number of classrooms for different subjects including gunnery, radar, wireless and Morse code. All the instructors were corporals or sergeants and extremely knowledgeable in their subjects.

In meteorology lessons we learned how to understand weather reports and the conditions and hazards you could expect to encounter from different cloud formations and weather fronts. The Meteorology Office sent out a specially equipped aircraft operated by a specialist crew daily to check the weather conditions all along the route we would be operating that night. These aircraft would climb up to 25,000ft recording weather conditions at fixed locations.

We also studied celestial navigation, as stars were an excellent method of navigating and an alternative back up plan if all else failed. We had to learn all the main stars used for navigational purposes such as Polaris (the North Star), Sirius and Mintaka.

Part of our training included how to operate the .303 calibre Browning machine gun to enable us to take over the position of mid-upper gunner or rear gunner, should an emergency arise. Thankfully, I never had to do this in combat, as it would probably have meant that one of my friends, Pete or Taffy, were injured or dead.

We all learned the basics of how to fly the aircraft just in case the pilot became incapacitated, but we all used to joke about this and came to the conclusion that if the pilot was incapacitated, it would probably be best to bail out! Thankfully, I never had to take over flying the aircraft.

At Yatesbury there was a parade ground with a flagpole in front of the station's headquarters, that was meant for square bashing, but we wasted very little time doing this as we were far too busy training. In fact, the only time you would see us participate in anything ceremonial was every Friday, when we would march down to the pay office and stand on parade. One by one they would call out our names and we would step forward shouting out the last three digits of our service number, at which point we would be handed our pay. Our sick bay and a church were also located in our headquarters. Thankfully I never required the sick bay, but I did attend the communion service every Sunday in church.

As our final exams drew near, we spent most of our leisure time testing one another. Our last few lectures included all of the latest information concerning the modern navigation systems such as the new H2S Mk11. This was the first airborne radar ground scanning system, which helped bomber crews identify targets on the ground for night and all-weather bombing. It was also extremely useful in aiding navigation, allowing landmarks to be identified at long range.

Finally, it was examination day. We all filed into a main hall; there were about 25 of us remaining at this final stage out of the original 40 who had started the course. It was a huge relief to finally sit our exams.

In the days following our exams, whilst we waited for the

results, we were all sent off base on various duties. Three of us were sent on guard duty. We were issued with two firearms, a tent, and some rations and told to guard Salisbury Plain. We were dropped off not far from Stonehenge. One could only hope that such an outstanding Neolithic Wonder of the World, would not be inadvertently destroyed by a German bomber, but there was not much we could do to protect it with two small pistols. Salisbury Plain covers approximately 300 square miles and is the largest Army Training Centre in Great Britain. I'm not sure how we were supposed to guard such a vast area against the potential threat of German parachutists, but we settled into our tent for the couple of days and carried out our guard duty.

I was very pleased with the outcome of the exams, especially when I received my Signaller (S) badge and was promoted from Trainee Aircrew to Aircrew Sergeant. Before joining a squadron, we were given a few days leave, but unfortunately this wasn't quite long enough for me to make the long journey home. For those of us unable to return to see our families, the RAF laid on some transport into the beautiful city of Bath. We spent two glorious days in Bath just being tourists and enjoying the sights and the sunshine. A highlight was visiting Sally Lunn's tearooms. I can still remember the beautiful cinnamon bun covered in icing, which I had there. It was the most delicious thing I had ever tasted. The Roman Baths turned its Pump Room into a dormitory with a number of beds fitted close together for the use of service personnel at a cost of one shilling per night. The Roman Baths were closed to the public, but we were taken on a detailed tour. Our tour guide explained that it had once been a magnificent Roman Temple and was unique because it had a natural flow of warm water. The rainfall off the Mendip Hills percolates deep down through limestone where geothermal energy raises the water temperature to about ninety degrees Celsius. The pressure of the heated water forces it to the surface and provides the Baths with a beautiful supply of naturally heated mineralised water. I really enjoyed my stay in Bath, but all too soon it was time to return to base.

CHAPTER 13

MOUNTAIN DODGING

T hose of us who passed the final exams were now transferred to RAF Millom near Barrow-in-Furness, Cumbria. It was late afternoon in January 1944 when we arrived and were told that a rescue party had just been sent out as one of its aircraft had crashed into the high ground nearby. All the rescue services were out, but we were told that, sadly, there was very little hope of anyone having survived. We had heard about such incidents occurring during training, often due to pilot or navigator error, appalling weather conditions or wireless failure. However it really brought it home to us, thinking of the poor trainees who had just lost their lives and not even made it into battle. During that evening, news drifted back that there were no survivors. It just seemed like such an incredible waste, that one simple mistake had led them to crash into a mountain. The Mountain Rescue team members were all local volunteers, both men and women of all ages, who were mountain climbers and first aiders. It must have been horrendous for those volunteers being the first on the scene of such accidents.

Whilst at RAF Millom our training would be conducted in an Avro Anson aircraft. This was a twin-engine multi-role air-training aircraft. The landing gear was usually left in the down position during training sorties, due to the laborious process which the pilot had to go through hand cranking the gear down into the locked position. There were four crew in the Anson and my operating station as the wireless operator was just behind the rear spar of the aircraft. This consisted of a table with all my wireless apparatus on it, including a winch for the trailing aerial, which was attached to the upper fuselage immediately behind the cockpit.

Our training consisted mainly of cross-country and navigational flights and classroom revision of the subjects in which we had already passed exams. However, it was an advanced, informative and enlightening course. We learned how small light aircraft were also an integral part of this war, used on aircraft carriers for dropping torpedoes and by the army and RAF to tow gliders. The single engine Westland Lysander, and aircraft similar to it were used to drop off and pick up special agents in France and Germany. These small aircraft could secretly cross the English Channel undetected and, due to their short landing and take-off capabilities, could land in small isolated fields. All the special agents had been selected for their individual skills. Some were wireless operators while a few were politicians, actors, and academics. A large majority of them were bilingual or multilingual. There were also a number of gifted technicians, experts in their fields, such as explosives. Some agents were dropped into occupied countries to help train resistance groups. There were various methods used to get instructions to these agents. Messages were often included in a British Broadcasting Corporation (BBC) Foreign Radio Service. The agent would be told to listen to this service every day for their pre-arranged signal such as: "The weather is expected to be sunny on Monday", meaning "Monday is the day to carry out your task". Other instructions were sent by Morse code to agents who had a secret radio receiver in their attic or small hideout. Agents would also travel into a neighbouring neutral country and go to a safe house for provisions, money and instructions for their next task. All these secret agents carried a cyanide capsule, which when taken was immediately fatal. There had been reports of agents being captured and subjected to brutal torture to extract information, before being hung or shot. Therefore, agents were encouraged to take a cyanide capsule rather than risk torture.

Whilst we sat in our lectures learning about all these covert operations, little did we know that this was exactly what was going on at that very moment in preparation for the D-Day landings. From 28th May until 23rd June 1944, all our training flights were scheduled as cross-country flight training. We didn't realise it at the time, but these sorties were being used as a decoy to confuse the enemy. Everything to do with D-Day required meticulous strategic planning and was kept top secret so that even the troops on the landing craft didn't know where they would be landing.

D-Day undoubtedly changed the fortunes of the war. On 6th June 1944, 160,000 Allied troops crossed the English Channel to Normandy as part of Operation Overlord. 12,000 aircraft and over 7,000 vessels transported thousands of troops to different beaches along a fifty-mile stretch of the Normandy coast. The 5th and 7th US Army landed at beaches that had been code-named Omaha and Utah. British and Canadian troops landed at beaches code-named Gold, Juno and Sword. Once the beaches were secure more troops were transported across to Normandy, until by the end of August there were more than three million Allied troops in Normandy. Battles raged on until finally the Nazi army retreated across the River Seine and the liberation of France was finally achieved by 25th August 1944.

The official news of the invasion was broadcast at 8am on 6th June 1944 and confirmed at 9:30am. General Eisenhower issued "Communique *Number One*" telling the French people that a landing had been made by our allies in Normandy. News of the invasion of France was further confirmed by King George VI when he broadcast to the British people urging them to pray for all those involved and for their success.

A lot of time was spent not only preparing for the actual

invasion, but also planning misleading manoeuvres. All Allied aircraft, like ours, not directly involved in the invasion, were used to distract and confuse the enemy into expecting attack from other directions. It was incredible that despite all the personnel involved in this covert operation nothing of significance was leaked to the enemy.

Whilst Operation Overlord was being carried out in Normandy we continued with our training at RAF Millom. On 11th June 1944 we made our first night flight in an Anson no. 68 flying for three hours and ten minutes. This gave all the crew a chance to use their skills at night. We completed 30 hours and 50 minutes flight training whilst at Millom. Most of the training flights went smoothly and we were steadily growing in confidence as a crew, but on our last training sortie we had to fly a cross-country route at night and we experienced a few close shaves. It really brought it home to us just how dangerous it could be flying at night, sometimes quite low, between and over mountains. Apparently one of the reasons Millom had been selected for training was to teach crews an awareness of terrain issues, but we felt that surely it would be better for inexperienced crews to gain more experience first before other navigational issues were added. We all agreed that it was not surprising there had been a few terrain accidents at Millom with most of them sadly being fatal. We were all pleased to leave RAF Millom still all in one piece. At this point I had accrued a total of 52 hours flying time of which six hours and ten minutes had been flown at night.

After our mountain dodging training at RAF Millom, we were next moved to the RAF station at Little Horwood in Buckinghamshire. On arrival we were shown into a large reception room. There were forty-eight of us, all recently qualified aircrew. The Station Commander introduced himself and welcomed us to our new base. He finished his introduction by saying:

"Right chaps I want you all to go out into the yard and sort yourselves into crews the best you can."

The pilots went around making up their crews of six members. Each Wellington bomber crew consisted of a pilot, navigator, bomb-aimer, wireless operator, flight engineer and a rear gunner. I happened to be standing next to Pilot Flying Officer Rogers, so he turned to me and asked if I'd like to be part of his crew. We were all complete strangers, but we all soon bonded together, shaking hands, friendly, cheerful and enthusiastic, as though we had known each other for years. There was no rank distinction apart from when we were in an aircraft when the pilot was recognised as being in sole charge. We all became good friends and worked incredibly well as a team.

Our original six-man crew remained together throughout the rest of the war and consisted of our pilot Flt Lt Eric C Rogers, our navigator Sgt J C Cole, our bomber aimer Flt Off D W Abercrombie, flight engineer Sgt Kenneth P Smale, myself Sgt J H Meller as the wireless operator and our rear gunner Sgt Peter Potter.

Whilst at Little Horwood we were trained to operate a Vickers Wellington, a medium weight long-range bomber aircraft, which was used as a good training aircraft in readiness for moving on to the Lancaster. The Wellington was the largest aircraft any of us had operated so far.

It was really nice to settle down to flying with the same crew members each day. We soon established a routine and really enjoyed working together as a crew. My operating station was in the centre of the aircraft. We had a training pilot flying with Flying Officer Rogers for the first five hours training and then after that, on 22nd July 1944, we did our first solo as a crew. This consisted of circuit practice, which is when you stay in the airport circuit going round and round just practising your take-offs, landings and overshoots. After that it was back to having a training pilot onboard again as we practised air-to-air and high-level bombing techniques and some night flying. We did our first solo at night as a crew on the Wellington on 6th August 1944.

On 16th August 1944 we were transferred the short distance down to RAF Wing to continue our flight training on the Wellington. Wing was near Aylesbury in Buckinghamshire. The motto on the wall in the mess was "Man is not Lost" and someone had written underneath it "but occasionally is uncertain of his exact location". Thankfully we never managed to become uncertain of our exact location during our practice cross country flights!

A few months later we transferred to RAF Woolfox Lodge in

Rutland, Leicestershire. Woolfox Lodge was a beautiful country estate. The manor house grounds had been commissioned by the RAF but sadly we didn't get to stay at the manor house; instead we were billeted in our usual Nissen huts in the grounds of the Lodge. Once we had settled into our huts, we were told to report to the uniform stores to be fitted for our individual combat flying suits. Our flying suits included beautifully crafted fur-lined leather boots and a fur-lined leather flying jacket, an oxygen mask and a floatation aid in case of ditching in the sea. I loved the feel, and even the smell of our flying suits with all the good quality soft leather. It was a fantastic, practical uniform and it felt good to wear. We all put on our new kit to check for sizing and our spirits were high as we teased and bantered about how smart we all looked in our new kit. We were a close-knit crew now, reliant on one another's skills and we all enjoyed the comradeship.

Our Nissen huts were a long way from the aircraft dispersal areas and so transport was laid on for us when we were on flight duty, but the rest of the time we had to walk back and forth or hitch a lift if we could.

RAF Woolfox Lodge was our last training base where we finally learned to operate the aircraft we would be flying in combat - the Avro Lancaster bomber. The Lancaster had an additional mid-upper gunner as well as a rear gunner and so a young Welsh lad, nicknamed Taffy joined our crew.

Our first training flight on a Lancaster bomber was on 6th December 1944 - registration BS-J. I can still remember my excitement as I approached the Lancaster for the first time. Those heavyweight four engine bombers were breathtaking; there was just something so majestic about them. Our Commander-in-Chief "Bomber" Harris referred to the Lancaster as his "shining sword". British newspapers were always championing the Lancaster bomber along with the Hurricane and the Spitfire fighters as the defenders of our airspace. It was a privilege to now be part of that fighting force.

We were scheduled for flight training most days during December and January on various forms of training sorties. When we weren't flying, we were still sent to do a daily check on one of the Lancasters. We would fire everything up to make sure it was in full working order. This not only checked that everything was fully functioning, but also kept us familiar with all the instruments and our pre-flight drills. The daily inspections were carried out first by the ground crew and then we would conduct our own checks afterwards. It was a belt and braces system to make sure nothing got missed.

The ground crews - flight mechanics, wireless mechanics, flight riggers, fitters and armourers, were all extremely well trained and dedicated to their jobs. They worked ridiculously long hours patching up the damaged aircraft and getting them ready to go back into combat. A close bond was usually built up between the ground crew and the aircrew, resulting in the occasional drink together. Aircrew were very much aware that their lives could depend on the expertise and efficiency of each ground crew member and their dedication was greatly appreciated and acknowledged.

Once the ground crew gave us the all clear to board the aircraft it was my job, as wireless operator, to check the aircraft batteries, the R1155 receiver and the T1154 transmitter as well as the location and serviceability of the Very pistol. Occasionally, we would watch each other checking our respective instruments, just in case it was necessary to take over if a member of the crew became incapacitated. I would observe all the crew members going through their tasks from time to time, but spent more time concentrating on the tasks and checks of the gunners and the navigator as those were the positions I would most likely have to take over.

The pilot and the flight engineer would work together checking the engine and flight instruments and controls. The pilot would do the external walk round, checking the flight controls, fuselage and engines externally, as well as the undercarriage and tyres.

As a crew, we all fell in love with the Avro Lancaster bomber aircraft and the man-made roar of those four Merlin engines. What an incredible sensation it was, poised at the end of the runway, listening to the mighty roar of those Merlins building up to full power ready for take-off and then feeling the kick in your back as they accelerated you forward and into the air. There was something so compelling about the sounds, the vibration of the airframe and even the smell of the inside of that aircraft which I shall never forget and will be forever grateful to have experienced. What a majestic aircraft the Lancaster was and how pleased I was to be part of its crew. We were at the cutting edge of technology in one of the world's greatest bombers and Adolf Hitler had better be ready.

CHAPTER 14

149 SQUADRON

In February 1945 we were finally deemed ready for combat and were transferred to join our first operational squadron at RAF Methwold in Norfolk.

As part of our welcome reception we were told a little bit about the squadron we were joining. The emblem of 149 Squadron was a horseshoe with a lightning strike through the centre. We were told that the horseshoe depicted the squadron's connection with the cavalry and it was also seen as a good luck symbol. The lightning strike (which didn't seem that desirable a charm for aircrew) had apparently been selected as being symbolic of speed and precision. The squadron motto was *"Fortis Nocte"* meaning "Strong by Night".

Once our welcoming speech was over, we were directed to

our Nissen hut accommodation, but as we entered, we were halted in mid stride by the sight of RAF military police solemnly emptying some of the bedside lockers that we were about to fill. We knew this meant that the crew we were replacing had failed to return, but nothing was said by anyone. The military police silently collected the personal belongings of some of the hut's previous occupants, while those still remaining carried on their routines and welcomed us in. We knew not to enquire or help, but nonetheless it was the elephant in the room. Once the RAF police had finished with the lockers, they headed for the car park to remove all the abandoned bicycles and cars, whose owners would not be returning. It was a stark reminder that the inside of a Lancaster was one of the most dangerous places to be during World War 2.

I settled onto my bed determined not to contemplate the fate of the previous occupant. The aircrew member in the bed opposite immediately engaged us in conversation in order to break the tension. He chattered on about how basic the British aircrew accommodation was; how we had all just grown to accept our Nissen huts, with their coal fired stoves in the middle, our outside chemical toilets and very basic washrooms. As my new room-mate pointed out, this was all in stark contrast to US aircrew, whose accommodation was far superior. Someone else then pointed out that the Americans were a long way from home, and we were all extremely grateful that they were here. We all contributed to the conversation and tried to forget the images we had just seen - the personal belongings of the previous aircrew being removed. To be honest, the lack of luxury in our accommodation was not my greatest concern, but I was very happy to have the distraction that this conversation offered.

We were given a couple of days to settle into our new base with only a few short briefings. During one of these we were informed that we would shortly be going into combat for the first time and that if we were unlucky enough to be captured, we would be entitled to certain rights under the Geneva Convention relating to our treatment as prisoners of war. Under interrogation you were only obliged to give your name, rank and service number. However, we were informed that there were many confirmed cases where the Nazis were not adhering to these regulations. We were also informed that as we were now operational crew, we would receive a small pay rise of a shilling a day. Looking back a shilling a day doesn't seem that significant as danger money, but I was very pleased to be receiving it at the time.

Before our first operational flight we were given a much-welcomed break of seven days leave. I wasted no time in making my way back home to Padgate. Obviously, I had no time to write and no other way to let my parents know I was coming home, but it was priceless seeing the look on my mother's face when I walked in. I was expecting my younger brother Herbert to be at home too, so I was shocked to hear that he had not only been called up into the army, but he had already been sent to join his regiment somewhere out in Europe.

The speed with which he had gone from civilian to the front line both startled and troubled me and was in stark comparison to my two years of training. It was even more worrying as my brother was the most unlikely soldier one would ever imagine. Herbert had such a kind nature and wouldn't harm a fly. I had always been there to protect him during our schooldays and I just couldn't begin to imagine how he was coping as a front line foot soldier. Seeing his belongings still around the house was strange. I missed him a great deal.

It was so nice to be home and just do as I pleased; to be back in my own room and able to sleep in as long as I liked in the mornings. My mother cooked me all my favourite meals and it was so lovely to go for a stroll down memory lane, revisit all my favourite childhood places and just enjoy the countryside. It was interesting to see how most people had turned their gardens into allotments. I took a couple of trips into Warrington, visited the market and looked around the shops and restaurants. I was shocked at how much Warrington had altered since my childhood. The traffic was now largely bicycles, or motorised vehicles, with only a few horse-drawn carts still about. I noticed that George Formby was back home between tours with the Entertainments National Service Association (ENSA) and was performing for his home audience at the Royal Court Theatre, so I decided to treat myself to a ticket. It was so relaxing sitting in the theatre listening to his cheerful fun-loving songs including: *Bless 'em All, When I'm Cleaning Windows, Leaning on a Lamp Post* and *With my little Ukulele in my Hand.* My extra wage meant I could enjoy treating myself; it just felt good to be home, having accomplished and experienced so much. It was really good to be able to meet old school friends, and catch up with all their news and share mine.

All too soon it was time for me to return to base, and for my mother this meant both her sons would now be in combat. As I said my goodbyes, my mother, with tears in her eyes, reminded me to always wear my St Christopher and to just take extreme care. Deep down, although no such words were ever spoken, I felt she must have realised, as I did, that this could easily be our last goodbye.

Whenever travelling on our own we were always told to wear our uniform as this meant that civilians would then do their very best to aid our journey in any way they could. I was always pleasantly surprised and humbled when total strangers would look at the aircrew badge on my uniform, smile and wish me "Good Luck". It made the risk I had volunteered to take as aircrew feel really appreciated.

When I returned to RAF Methwold, it felt good to be back with the rest of the crew, and catch up with all their news.

I can still clearly remember the early morning sounds and routines of an operational air force base in 1945. It was February so the mornings were very chilly, but the stove in the centre of our hut kept us comfortably warm. The first man up would stoke the fire and add some more coal from the scuttle. I was never the first man up; I would always stay in my bed as long as possible. As I woke up, I'd hear the other aircrew waking up around me. My routine was to have a wash and a shave, get into my normal uniform and then we'd all wander up, as a crew, to the mess for breakfast together - except for the officers who stayed in separate accommodation. In our crew the pilot and the bomb aimer were both officers. The camaraderie was excellent and no distinction was made of rank when we flew together, we just worked as a team, the only main distinction was that officers had better living accommodation and a separate mess. I think generally, most crews would have preferred to stay together and on one occasion I remember hearing that an officer had been given a warning for trying to dine with the rest of his crew rather than dining in the officers' mess. After breakfast we would normally meet up with the two officers by the noticeboard, where we went every morning to see if our crew was listed for operational flying that night.

I can still remember seeing our crew's names on the rota for the first time; it was 16th February 1945 and the aircraft we would be operating was NG261/OJ-E.

CHAPTER 15

INTO COMBAT

After two years of studying, tests, exams, fitness work and flight training, the moment for action had finally arrived. Our first combat flight was on 16th February 1945 and I was 20 years old.

It cost in the region of £10,000 to train each crew member and each Lancaster bomber cost the government approximately £45,000 to manufacture. We were an expensive, highly trained weapon, all we could hope for now was that we didn't end up as a wasted resource.

Most Lancaster bombing raids were carried out under the cover of night and we were scheduled for an afternoon departure, to arrive over the destination at dusk on a dark February evening. After lunch we started to get ourselves ready for the mission. The back of a Lancaster bomber was a chilly place to be, as the temperature cools significantly with altitude so even on a summer's day the temperature at altitude was cold. There was no heating in the aircraft, apart from the electrically heated suit that the rear gunner wore and plugged in. The rear gunner's turret was very exposed to the elements and there were a lot of draughts as the turrets had to be manoeuvrable in order to swing the guns around at an enemy fighter. Even right in the centre of the Lancaster where I was stationed was generally freezing at altitude. I would always wear a thick pair of pyjamas under my uniform trousers and a couple of vests. I had three sets of flannelette pyjamas, one for bed, one for combat and the other set in the wash.

Before every operational flight there was always a full briefing, led by our Wing Commander and Station Commander; it was here that we would learn the intended target for the first time. The target was disclosed on a need-to-know basis only as it was imperative that the enemy didn't get advance warning about the location. We were then given the coordinates for the rendezvous point, which was normally over the North Sea, (it was just the coordinates which altered).

Sir Arthur Harris, the Commander in Chief of Bomber Command, employed what he called "a thousand bomber tactics" for the majority of his planned air raids, which meant getting as many heavy bombers in formation as possible. We rarely managed anywhere near one thousand, but nonetheless there was always a formidable formation that would rendezvous before an attack. Bomber Command was made up of six Groups and each Group had a number of Squadrons occupying different airfields and each Squadron had two or three Flights. At full strength each Flight had about eight aircraft, but sadly we were rarely at full strength. Bomber Harris' technique was a successful war tactic, as our combined might meant that there was usually little left of the designated target by the time we had all emptied our bomb bays and returned to base.

That afternoon we were instructed to fly at a height of 18,000ft at all times (it was usually between 18,000ft and 21,000ft). Other bases would be given different altitudes to separate us and try to avoid collisions. We would have preferred a higher altitude, as at the lower altitudes there was always the increased risk of being underneath another bomber when it released its bombs.

The briefing included the most likely areas en-route where we could expect to come under a barrage of anti-aircraft guns. Our target that night was Wesel, which we ended up bombing four times over a period of five nights; our crew went on all four of these bombing raids. Next we were given the most up-to-date information available concerning the weather. We soon learned that these reports were not to be relied upon, but at least they gave us some idea of cloud levels particularly over the target. Next, we were given any other information that may be helpful concerning the target and its location, normally gleaned from intelligence officers working behind enemy lines. Finally, the officer in charge of the briefing would wish us all "Good Luck".

After the briefing we went down the hallway to the store to collect our parachute and our Mae West (an inflatable life jacket in the form of a collar, extending down the chest). These life jackets were given this nickname after the American actress, sex symbol and comedian Mae West. The store manager also cheekily asked if I still had my "full escape kit". I looked at him quizzically and then he pointed to the little button stitched to our tunics which was a cleverly designed compass to be used if we bailed out or crashed in enemy territory. Everything was kept as upbeat as possible to keep morale high. When one of our crew was collecting his parachute, he asked the pretty, young WAAF behind the desk: "What happens if I have to jump and this thing doesn't open?" Her immediate response was: "Don't worry about that, just bring it back and I'll exchange it for another one."

We then made our way out to catch the transport that would convey us around the perimeter to the dispersal where our Lancaster was being prepared ready for flight. There was always a hive of activity around the aircraft with ground crew carrying out their final checks, refuellers pumping in the designated fuel for the trip, and the bomb crews gently loading our payload of bombs into the bomb bays. It was then that I got my first rush of adrenaline running through every nerve in my body, a feeling of being alert and waiting.

My thoughts were racing with all the information we had just been given and the task that lay ahead; looking for the position of the moon, the cloud types and height and thinking through what I had to do as soon as we were given permission to board.

On that first operational flight I can remember standing silently on the dispersal waiting. I could hear some of the ground crew near me having a bet between themselves as to which target in Germany we would be bombing. They were estimating the weight of the bombs and the amount of fuel that we had in the tanks. They were betting three pence each. A few of them glanced cheekily in our direction hoping to get a hint that their guess was correct, but no one offered any clues. Our lives and the lives of all of our fellow aircrew standing by at that moment to get airborne, at airfields all around Great Britain, depended on us keeping the target a closely guarded secret.

The chief ground engineer gave our pilot the nod and then our pilot gave us the command to board. One by one we clambered up the short metal ladder at the side of the Lancaster. I can remember feeling shivery and not being sure if it was the chill of February or the rush of adrenaline. We shuffled our way along to our positions and then in silence started our individual checklists. The routine and the discipline of our procedures kept us all centred on our task. The pilot called each of us on the intercom to check we were all ready and then, one by one, the four engines roared into life. The pilot then signalled "chocks away" to the ground crew and we were on our way, taxiing along the perimeter to join the other Lancasters awaiting their turn to get airborne. It was an incredible sight and sound and I felt exhilarated to be part of it. The sound of all those Merlin engines idling along the taxiways was incredible.

As we gathered speed along the runway, we could see a number of ground crew and non-flying aircrew waving us off on our mission, and as we rose over the hedgerows, civilians on the roadside and in their gardens were waving too. It was incredible how this small act of respect and wishing us luck made the risk we were taking seem worthwhile.

As we climbed steadily with a heavy bomb load below, the navigator took a few minutes to plot the course to our rendezvous point over the North Sea which he then handed over to the pilot. The navigator then started to calculate the route from the rendezvous to the target. On reaching a height of 10,000 feet, the pilot instructed all the crew to put on their oxygen masks. If any of us had to move around inside the aircraft once we were above this height, (as I had to do on a few occasions), we had to transfer as quickly as possible to another oxygen point in the aircraft. At higher altitudes you only had about five minutes of useful consciousness before the lack of oxygen would make you a bit dazed and less likely to complete the task. If you didn't then plug into the oxygen you could pass out.

Our flight out to the rendezvous point over the North Sea took us about half an hour and as we approached the allocated coordinates, we could see the other squadrons approaching in various formations from other directions.

Having reached the rendezvous point, we had been briefed to immediately alter course for our target of Wesel in Germany.

I can remember that first sortie so clearly. It was a beautiful evening and despite my nerves I couldn't help but enjoy watching the sunset and seeing the darkness closing in around the majesty of a legion of Lancasters.

We crossed the French coast and soon experienced our first attack from anti-aircraft guns. First you would see the searchlights lighting up the sky; you couldn't hear the guns, but next you would just see lots of black puffs and red flashes like a high-altitude firework display as the incendiary devices exploded around the aircraft. The aircraft would rock from the explosions. It was a surreal experience and, in those moments, I would often find myself holding on to the St Christopher my mother had given me. I would also find myself praying fervently too.

We had been briefed to drop the radar-jamming device known as Window at certain points en-route. It was the bomb aimer's job to drop the Window and he started to release our first batch immediately as the first searchlight lit up the sky and our formation. It was at this point I witnessed my first aircraft plummeting in flames. Sadly, this was the first of many, even on this trip alone. The Window soon took effect and the anti-aircraft guns lost their sighting and ceased firing.

We reached the next point at which we had been instructed to drop more Window and then all braced ourselves as it was obvious that this would be the next onslaught of anti-aircraft attack from the ground. The attack lasted for a few minutes before the Window took effect again, but sadly not before another Lancaster had been caught in the fire. In the main it was completely random as to which aircraft got hit and therefore mainly down to chance, but we felt that there was a tendency for the aircraft bringing up the rear to have a greater casualty rate so our crew made a note to stay in the middle of the main formation at all times.

As we got nearer to the coordinates of the target, we all started looking out for the pathfinder flares that indicated the point to drop our bombs. It wasn't too difficult for us to spot as by the time we approached the target, the ground below looked like a volcano had erupted.

Flying in tight formation with such large numbers of bombers brought to mind a flock of birds, especially when we reached the target. We'd all swoop in on the specified point and then, all moving, as one, we would pull out and turn for home, just like a murmuration of starlings. Collisions sadly did take place, but given the quantity of aircraft all in close proximity it was amazing how rarely this happened, especially as we had to maintain complete radio silence.

Our bomb aimer lay down in the front of the aircraft and directed the pilot on the intercom, saying "port one" (left) "starboard one" (right) until we reached the target. As we got closer to the target, the pilot opened the bomb doors and on the bomb aimer's instruction released the bombs. The bomb aimer then watched to make sure the bombs had been released before the pilot retracted the bomb bay doors and then came the very welcome words, "bombs gone- let's go home".

Once the bombs were dropped, we literally turned for home and set off as quickly as possible. The Lancaster's top speed when empty of bombs was about 270mph (434kmph). One of our greatest concerns was looking out for possible collisions with our Allied aircraft, but of course we still had to fly back through anti-aircraft fire on the way home too.

It was an incredible feeling as we crossed the English Channel back into British airspace.

We landed back at Methwold in the dark at about 6pm, safe and sound, having completed our first operational flight. The relief was incredible, but we didn't celebrate, we just went through the shutdown drills and then got our transport back to headquarters ready for our debriefing. All the time our eyes and ears were alert waiting for the possible return of other aircraft. We handed back our parachutes and Mae Wests in the storeroom and then went and sat down in the briefing room. The aircraft would arrive back in dribs and drabs so sometimes there would be a couple of crews debriefed together; other times we would be debriefed on our own. That afternoon we were debriefed alone. We headed for the mess, which was eerily quiet, to have some food and then went back to our Nissen hut. I remember being completely exhausted as I stripped down to my flannelette pyjamas; this time I didn't even bother to change them, I just sank into my bed. As exhausted as I was there were still those moments of reflection where images cluttered my sleepy brain, everything from Lancasters falling as fire balls from the sky to the red explosions of the anti-aircraft fire lighting up the interior of the aircraft. I'd stir in my half-sleep still subconsciously listening out for any other returning aircraft and their crew to fill the ominously empty beds in our Nissen hut. Despite these images, sleep finally engulfed me.

The next morning, I woke up and noted that the beds opposite were still un-slept in and that the chap who was normally the early riser, who stoked the stove and added the extra coal, must have been the occupier of one of them. As I peered over my sheets and took stock, I could see that it was only our crew still in the hut. I had almost resolved to get up and stoke the fire myself when I noticed Pete getting up to do the same. We chatted happily, completely avoiding the subject of the empty beds, but I did make time for a quick prayer of thanks and earnestly studied my St Christopher.

It wasn't until we headed into the mess for breakfast and saw all the empty chairs and empty tables that we realised just how many had tragically failed to return.

All those young talented men lost, most of them finishing their short lives in a plummeting fireball with their Lancaster. These were not thoughts you could harbour when you knew that soon you would be going out to do the same task again, and so our conversation remained firmly focused on the trivia of life, the fun and the banter of youth. No one mentioned it, but it was obvious that a lot of the tables and chairs had been removed and the remainder spread out in order to reduce the feeling of emptiness in the dining hall. Our mood only lifted when we met up with our pilot and bomb aimer and they informed us that we would not be operating that evening. It was a chilly morning and we would normally have returned to the warmth of our Nissen hut fire, but as we glanced across, we could see the RAF police were in our hut obviously removing the personal possessions from the bedside lockers of those who would never return to claim them. None of us said a word, but collectively decided to stay in the mess for a while instead. Returning to the newly made up beds that now awaited the next intake of fresh aircrew was hard too, but still none of us addressed the situation. You soon learnt that some subjects were just too abhorrent to even acknowledge, they would eat you up and destroy you if you dwelled on them, so instead we focused on playful banter, letters from home, every-day routine, drills and youthful resilience to keep us going.

We had one day off and then we were back out on the same route to bomb Wesel for the next three evenings. Each time the losses were high, but thankfully not as horrendous as they had been on our first operational bombing run.

Our next target after Wesel was on 22nd February in Osterfeld, Germany. We had just dropped our bombs in the early dusk and were setting our course for home when suddenly the aircraft searchlights caught us in their sights. Immediately we became a sitting duck and all the anti-aircraft guns were set on us. Our aircraft pitched and shuddered under the attack as our pilot dived to increase speed and turned us violently out of the searchlight and into cloud cover. His quick thinking saved us, but nonetheless we had already sustained a great deal of damage.

One engine was on fire and you could see the numerous holes in the fuselage from the flak damage. Thankfully, the engine fire went out as soon as the engine was shut down, but it meant returning home on three engines. We made it back to base without further incident, but on landing we were all amazed, as were the ground crew, at seeing the amount of damage that had been caused. The aircraft had been hit several times by flak but in one area a huge section of fuselage was completely missing and the aircraft was literally in tatters, yet amazingly we had all survived, completely unscathed. The aircraft PB138 was written off and destined for use as spare parts; we always felt a huge sadness when we knew an aircraft that had saved our lives was about to be scrapped.

New faces came and went from our hut. Sadly, aircrew were easier to replace than the aircraft, so for a while our base would be down to only a few aircraft until a fresh batch of newly manufactured Lancasters could be delivered. The Avro aircraft factory was kept overwhelmingly busy producing Lancasters as the rate of loss was so high. If an aircraft managed 500 hours flight time before being lost in action it was a rarity.

I didn't ever see the pilots who delivered the aircraft from the factory but often they were young women. Women were not allowed to operate in combat, but were actively employed to do all other duties. It was incredulous to me to think of women pilots delivering Lancaster bombers, as before the war, in my childhood community, it never occurred to anyone to suggest that a woman should have a go at driving a lorry, a tractor and certainly not an aircraft. There is little doubt that World War 2 was a huge turning point for women's liberation and I'm extremely proud to say that years later, my own daughter Caroline, became an Airline Captain for British Regional Airlines.

My last visit home to see my mother before combat.

Our Lancaster's cockpit.

Taxiing out to the main runway. Other squadron aircraft and the main hangars in the distance.

View back toward the airfield, just after take-off.

My wireless station (foreground left), with a view forward to the cockpit.
The bomb aimer's position can be glimpsed at bottom-right.

A formation of Lancasters of 207 Squadron.
The two aircraft at right are EM-G and EM-C, respectively.

A formation of Lancasters of 115 Squadron.
The Lancaster at foreground-right is KO-E.

CHAPTER 16

GENERAL DOGSBODY

People often ask me what my task was as a wireless operator on board a Lancaster bomber and my quick response is that I was the general dogsbody.

The pilot was obviously the person in charge of the aircraft and the crew. Interestingly this was irrespective of rank, but other than that distinction, we all worked as a crew and relied heavily on the skills of each member. All the different tasks were very clearly defined, except for my job as the wireless operator. The most obvious overlap was helping the navigator. We sat very close to each other, as our jobs were co-dependent. I would assist the navigator by tuning in any ground navigation beacons along our route, using the aircraft loop aerial, and then identify them using the Morse code identification signal which was transmitting from the beacon at all times. Once I had identified the ground beacon, I would pass this information to the navigator for him to take the bearings and plot our position and course. It was important to establish fixed position reports at regular intervals, so that whenever the pilot needed it, the navigator could call out a heading change and provide our current location.

Telegraphy was not as sophisticated or reliable as it is today, so in order to maintain radio contact with our operational base, I would have to monitor the frequency on my R1154 receiver and listen for any changes in our target or flight plan. On one occasion near the end of the war, I received an urgent Morse code message "Change of Target". It turned out that our troops had advanced much faster than expected and had now captured and secured the targeted area, so not only was there no need to bomb it but had we missed that Morse code message we would have been bombing our own troops.

Radio signals relied on the Heaviside layer; a layer of naturally occurring ionised gas about 60 miles above the Earth's surface, which forms one of the several gas layers in the ionosphere. Oliver Heaviside was one of the first scientists who theorised that radio waves may be able to be propagated beyond the horizon, by bouncing them off this ionised gas. In 1924, an English physicist, Edward Appleton first proved Heaviside's theory to be correct by running a series of experiments. He later won the Nobel Prize for Physics in 1947 for this work. He proved that medium length frequency waves radiated into the sky from one area would be reflected back from the ionosphere down to Earth a long distance away. This method of sky wave or skip method was used for radio communication throughout the war. The skip distance of radio waves alters at night, as the ionised gas moves slightly further away from the Earth's surface during the evening and night, making the medium wave radio signals travel further at night. As most of our flights were conducted at dusk, I would often have to retune the radio as the sun began to set in order to maintain radio contact. The Heaviside layer is also slightly affected by seasonal temperature changes and sunspot activity but, despite all of this, in the main, wireless telegraphy was very efficient, although it was a time-consuming task.

Very high frequency (VHF) radios were introduced towards the end of the war and provided a much clearer, consistent form of radio communication. However, VHF could only be used over short distances as the high frequency radio waves penetrated straight through the Heaviside layer and were not reflected back down to Earth. VHF therefore became the radio wave of choice for short distance communication and medium wave (MW) was used to communicate over longer distances.

All wireless operators were trained how to use an Aldis lamp, which had a trigger-operated shutter. We hardly ever used this, but it was there in case we needed to communicate by Morse code semaphore with another aircraft in formation with us, whilst maintaining radio silence. I can remember using it once in flight on our way out on a night time operation over

Germany. We saw a number of US Flying Fortress Bomber aircraft B-17 returning from a successful daytime bombing raid, so we signalled them by Aldis lamp to say "Well Done" to which we received the reply "Good Luck."

All crew members were trained in first aid, but it tended to be the wireless operator who looked after the injured. There was a morphine bottle with a syringe kept in our first aid kit in case of emergency. We were lectured on the importance of using only a minimum dose, as too much could be fatal. Thankfully I was never required to administer morphine.

If the pilot declared that the aircraft would have to ditch in the sea, all the crew would assemble ready to evacuate, except for the wireless operator, who had to remain at his station sending out a mayday signal, for as long as possible, in order to increase the chances of being rescued by passing ships or rescue services. The pilot and I knew that if we had to ditch in water we would be the last ones out.

My station on board a Lancaster was situated not too far from the bomb bay, so if the pilot requested, I was the one sent to make sure all of our bombs had been safely released. Occasionally, you would get a hung bomb, (one that had decided to cling on and was now half in and half out of the aircraft). If this happened the bomb release button had to be pressed again. Fortunately, ours always dropped on the second release!

If the pilot wanted an assessment of damage to the rear of the aircraft once the immediate danger had passed, it would always be me who would be sent. On the return flight from one operation we came under heavy attack from German fighter aircraft. There was a full battle ensuing around us; both our gunners were whirling around shooting at the attacking aircraft. There were both Focke-Wulfe 190s and Messerschmitts in the vicinity, but we had one Focke that just would not leave us alone. Our Lancaster sustained a great deal of damage, but finally, the fighter turned away. We were pretty certain that our gunners had damaged it. We got back to our base without further issue but immediately after landing, our pilot discovered he was unable to steer the aircraft on the ground. This must have been due to damage caused to the controls during the attack. The aircraft skidded and went off the runway onto the grass and finally came to a bumpy halt. We all clambered out unscathed and had to leave our abandoned Lancaster to the ground engineers to sort out.

Most of the aircraft that made it back to base were damaged; some would go in for repair, but many had to be scrapped for parts. The ground engineers were fantastic at patching up the aircraft and we would soldier on with minor defects. However, on one occasion, we had just set off for a training flight when we developed a substantial oil leak from the outer starboard engine so had to shut it down. We couldn't return to Methwold as we had too much fuel on board and the extra weight meant we needed a much longer stopping distance on landing and therefore a longer runway. I sent a message to our Operations and they told us to divert to RAF Valley on the Isle of Anglesey, in North West Wales.

We made a safe landing at RAF Valley and then remained there for two days, whilst repair work was carried out on our Lancaster. RAF Valley was a very interesting base, as it was also used as a ferry base for the USAAF. We were made very welcome, but we were all astounded by the contrast between the US aircrew's way of life compared to ours. Their accommodation was much more comfortable and relaxing. It was just small details, but added up, they made a big difference to your comfort and feeling of wellbeing. For instance, there were no Nissen huts - just purpose-built accommodation and each bed had a bedside lamp. Their mess was much better laid out with a good selection of meals to choose from, and with no limit on how much you could have.

The atmosphere was very relaxed at RAF Valley although, to be fair, we had noticed that the RAF was generally trying to relax some of its protocols by introducing a no drill, no inspections, no pulling of rank policy for operational aircrew. It was a big topic of conversation for our crew, because we all felt that discipline was essential. We all acknowledged that our strength as a crew relied on each of us being very self-disciplined and we all just took it for granted that each of us would always give of his best. This meant maintaining a very high level of efficiency and fitness, not only for your own safety, but also for the safety of every member of your crew. Our conclusion was that good initial training required tough discipline, but once a crew member had truly learned the meaning of self-discipline, it was nice to have extraneous protocols a little more relaxed, which was what we noticed during our stay at RAF Valley.

I always joked that I was just the general dogsbody, but on one occasion, on 14th April 1945, I had a chance to really put my skills to the test.

On 14th April we were sent on a raid to bomb the railway marshalling yards at Potsdam, just outside Berlin. Flying over Berlin, (the headquarters of the Third Reich), was obviously one of the most precarious operational flights we made. Berlin and Potsdam were the most heavily guarded areas anywhere in Germany, shielded by a huge array of radar-assisted searchlights and anti-aircraft guns, so that the whole sky seemed to light up. In addition, any aircraft caught flying anywhere near Berlin could expect the full might and power of the Luftwaffe fighters defending their home territory.

Sadly, on every operational flight you would endure the horrific sight of several Lancasters going down in a ball of flames, or in an uncontrollable dive, or just completely exploding in the air. It was horrible to see a neighbouring aircraft suddenly light up, caught in the powerful brilliance of the searchlights, which would make the aircraft appear to freeze in the sky next to you. Next you would see myriad tiny explosions surrounding it from the anti-aircraft guns that sent up a curtain of high-powered explosive shells. Each shell would appear like a black puffball followed by red-hot razor-sharp shrapnel, cutting through the metal fuselage causing damage to equipment and injury or death to members of the crew. Some were lucky and escaped the snare of the searchlights but, sadly, many did not.

I think we all used to hold our breath as we closed in on a target. We were at our most vulnerable during those moments. As the bomb aimer gave his instructions it was impossible to take any evasive action to avoid the network of searchlights as they swept the skies, nor to avoid the anti-aircraft shells as they exploded close by. The concentration was tangible, as there was no point us flying through all that jeopardy if we didn't get a direct hit on the target. We would all sit in silence waiting for the words "bombs gone". The aircraft, now much lighter, would pitch up and the pilot would then point the nose of the aircraft downwards and wait a few seconds for the on-board camera to take a photograph of the target and the devastation below. As soon as that was complete the pilot would turn the aircraft for home and the navigator would give him the heading. The loss of Allied aircraft and their crew was always extremely high on raids over or near Berlin. Even so, it always felt worthwhile to be bombing the very heart of Hitler's might.

On this occasion, we had just successfully dropped our bombs, when the searchlights caught us in their sights. We were suddenly fully lit up and we could all see one another clearly. We knew we were now a sitting duck and that at that moment all the anti-aircraft guns would be swivelling into position and focusing on us. There were a few seconds of eerie quiet and then the explosions started all around us. You could hear, feel and see shrapnel tearing into the fuselage. The navigator's compartment suddenly burst into flames and so did the inner port engine; the interior of the aircraft shone brightly from our internal fire. The navigator and I grabbed the fire extinguishers and managed to extinguish the fire as the aircraft pitched and shuddered from the disturbance of the shells.

Then came the dreaded words from our pilot: "*STAND BY AND BE READY TO BAIL OUT.*" Apart from the pilot who was still in the cockpit steering the plane, and the rear gunner who would fall out backwards once he rotated the turret, the rest of the crew lined up near the exit door, all of us with our parachute on. There was no panic, just an awareness that death was almost inevitable. A crew check had already been made by the pilot - which he normally did in any kind of emergency.

We all knew there was little chance of surviving the parachute drop. We'd all done our training, but none of us were experienced. We were at about 18,000 feet where the temperature outside was freezing. We would have to remove our oxygen masks to jump and then hope that we could stay alert enough to count to allow the free fall without oxygen to about 10,000 feet, before opening the parachute.

Despite the horror, you couldn't help but be mesmerised by the drama of it all; the night sky lit by the searchlights, the anti-aircraft explosions, coloured flares dropped by the pathfinders and the furnace of the stricken target. It was like being part of some macabre firework display. The smoke from the fires rose thousands of feet into the night sky. It literally felt like the old saying of having to choose between "the frying pan and *the fire.*"

If any of us were fortunate enough to survive the free fall and pull our chutes, there was every chance of being sucked into the huge furnace that we had just created.

It is surprising how in just a few minutes between life and death one's whole life emerges. I can recall touching the St Christopher charm that was around my neck and having a strange feeling of relief. I was once again a child standing at the large white gates and being refused admission by an angel. I could clearly see all the members of my family and thought of how they would react to the news of my death.

Those moments seemed like an eternity with all odds stacked against us; moments that one can never forget however much one tries. Believing my time had come, and without realising it, I was silently reciting the Lord's Prayer:

"Our Father which art in Heaven, Hallowed be thy name, Thy Kingdom Come. Thy will be done ..."

I could hear the rattle of shrapnel on the fuselage and bomb doors and the Lancaster was shuddering violently,

" ... on Earth, as it is in Heaven. Give us this day our daily bread. And forgive us our trespasses, as we forgive those who trespass against us ..."

The searchlight that had held us in its sights suddenly went out and we plunged into darkness. The anti-aircraft shells that had been exploding all around us stopped, due no doubt to the anti-aircraft gun being hit by the bombs still being released by our colleagues. In the meantime, our pilot had managed to shut down and feather the port inner engine, which put out the engine fire. Once this engine was shut down all the shuddering stopped and the Lancaster was now properly back under control,

"… and lead us not into temptation, but deliver us from evil …"

The pilot told us to return to our seats as he put the aircraft into a steep dive which enabled it to gather speed. Miraculously, we were still flying, although we had sustained considerable damage and numerous mechanical faults

"For thine is the Kingdom, the power and the glory for ever and ever. Amen."

There had been a reasonably clear sky over the target, but on leaving the area we encountered cloud that got more and more dense as we travelled further away from the target. The cloud was our final salvation for the mid-upper gunner had observed a German Messerschmitt BF109 fighter aircraft in the distance circling around, waiting to pounce on an unfortunate disabled aircraft like ours. Protected by the cloud, the pilot turned on a heading roughly in the direction of home.

I breathed a sigh of relief, and silently said a prayer of thanks. It was now time to take stock of all the damage caused. Throughout this whole terrifying experience, we not only lost our bearings, but the fire had also destroyed all of the navigator's equipment. I managed to return to my station and worked away steadily with the loop aerial, until finally I picked up a signal and identified it. We set course towards that signal and I, again, used the loop aerial to pick up various radio stations and their bearings that I passed to the navigator to plot our position and navigate our way home.

Most of the flight back to base was through thick cloud with plenty of turbulence and the faithful Lancaster was creaking and groaning; it was not a pleasant journey. The landing was going to be difficult because of the damage to the controls and we swerved several times before finally coming to a stop. We had made it back and we were all safe with no injuries. Despite our relief to be home, we all felt sad to walk away from Lancaster "G" for George, which had somehow managed to limp home and save all our lives. We had been airborne for eight hours and 35 minutes, flying all through the night from our take-off at 20:26 until finally landing back at base at 05:01 the next morning. We knew we were very tight on fuel, but an engineer later told us that we had landed with only fumes remaining in the tank. It was obvious that Lancaster "G" was now well beyond repair and destined to be stripped for parts so before leaving it we all lingered for a while and gave it a pat. We could see the look of disbelief on the faces of the ground crew as they looked at the wreck of the aircraft and, spontaneously, they all started to applaud.

We had done well to get back to base. The pilot did a tremendous job of getting us out of a deadly combat situation, managing to control the damaged aircraft, the engine fire as well as looking after his crew. Shortly after this event he was deservedly promoted to Squadron Leader. The pilot and other members of the crew were also extremely complimentary about how well I'd coped, by obtaining loop aerial bearings to navigate our way home. Of course, the compliments only lasted a short while before all the playful banter started again.

CHAPTER 17

EMPTY CHAIRS AND EMPTY TABLES

B anter helped us cope with the sorrow, stress and fear. One mealtime I glanced across at a bomb aimer from one of the other crews. He was normally very cheerful and quick-witted, but today he looked very glum and close to tears. He had just finished reading a letter, which as usual during those days, had been long delayed in arriving and was over a month old. It was from his mother, who explained that their home had been completely destroyed by an air raid attack and that they were currently homeless. Tragically his dog had been killed too. They had tried to take the dog with them to the shelter, but he had panicked when he heard the sirens and had run off and hidden somewhere in the house. There had been no time to search for him and he had still been in the house when a German V1 rocket hit it. His parents had fortunately both survived. Even though the air raid shelter they were in sustained a lot of damage, it still managed to protect the lives of those inside. His parents wanted him to know, as they were never sure when he might come home on leave and didn't want him to return to a pile of rubble. They were hoping to be re-homed shortly and said they would write to let him know their new address as soon as they could.

This poor aircrew member was not alone; such stories were commonplace with people loosing not only their homes, but sadly their friends, much loved pets and even their families in the air raids. It was always extremely distressing as in essence this was what we were all fighting to protect and we all lived for that triumphant return home to the open arms of our families and the familiar warmth of our own rooms.

It was in moments like this that RAF banter came into play. As though on cue, three other members of his crew who were sitting alongside him, pushed their chairs back and lifted him aloft on his chair, shouting "Chair (cheer) Up!". All three men rose and put their arms around his shoulder and expressed their sorrow about the news, as did I and other members of our crew. We all then reminded him that at least his parents were still alive and everything would sort itself out. Then, the banter would start, with promises to get their revenge that night and to take him out for drinks, "we'll pay now you're homeless". Crew members tended to form very close friendships, loyalty and fellowship very quickly, as we were all in this incredibly precarious situation together. We knew that our life expectancy was extremely low, so we were all determined to enjoy life whilst we still could.

A week later, I glanced across the table at breakfast at seven empty chairs and the sad realisation hit me that his crew had failed to return from the air raid the night before. I remember thinking at least he was home now, and hopefully his dog was there to greet him. Years later I remember hearing the song from the stage show Les Misérables in which the lyrics struck home very hard:

There's a grief that can't be spoken
*   There's a pain goes on and on*
Empty chairs at empty tables
*   Now my friends are dead and gone*

Oh my friends, my friends forgive me
*   That I live and you are gone*
There's a grief that can't be spoken
*   There's a pain goes on and on.*

A few days later, I returned to the dining room to find those chairs filled again with fresh, brave, young faces. Something we never discussed, but were very aware of, was that we were now becoming an extremely rare phenomenon, as somehow we were managing to survive against all odds. We were now recognised as being one of the most experienced bomber crews

Our crew with lucky aircraft 'D for Dog'. From left to right: Sgt Kenneth Smale (flt eng), Sgt Peter Potter (rear gunner), Flt Lt Eric Rogers (pilot), myself (w op), Sgt J C Cole (nav), Flt Off D W Abercrombie, (bomb aimer) / Sgt E S 'Taffy' Campbell (mid-upper gunner).

On the wing: myself (w op) Sgt E S 'Taffy' Campbell (mid-upper gunner).
In front row from left to right: Sgt Peter Potter (rear gunner), Sgt Kenneth Smale (flt eng), Flt Lt Eric Rogers (pilot), Sgt J C Cole (nav), Flt Off D W Abercrombie (bomb aimer).

in 149 Squadron and as such, new recruits were keen to ask our advice and learn from our experience.

The reason we were surviving as a crew, was mainly down to good fortune, but there were a few factors that helped increase the odds in our favour. We were all very good at our tasks and we all worked hard at staying fit and alert and looking after our general health. My old boxing coach's favourite mantra *"mens sana in corpore sana"* ("a sound mind in a healthy body") always remained with me. Each phase of a flight could catch out the unwary - from take-off to landing. Crew illness, fatigue, even burst tyres cost lives, so we worked hard to rule out as many of these aspects as we could control. Sometimes our battle against the weather was almost as dramatic as our battle against the Nazis. The turbulence was so atrocious the aircraft would rock around almost completely out of control. At other times the outside temperature would drop dramatically, with ice forming on the wings with the possibility it could freeze on the propellers and engine intakes, as well as the aircraft controls. We passed on all these tips, but after that it was all just simply down to luck.

If we were a lucky crew, there was also the odd aircraft that was lucky too. "X" for X-Ray and "D" for Dog, managed to keep returning raid after raid with different crews. Each aircraft had a different slogan painted on the side of the fuselage "D" for Dog had "Right Over Might" painted on it with a large white cross painted over the top of a Nazi Swastika. A photographer visited RAF Methwold and several crews had a photo taken next to "D" for Dog. This aircraft had completed 43 raids when the photo was taken in 1945. I don't recall how many it managed in total, but I do know that it managed to survive the war.

As we stood on the dispersal before each flight, waiting for the ground crew to finish their tasks, we would often pass the time and relieve the tension by studying the clouds and debating what type they were and the flying conditions we could expect from them. Some clouds would help us by giving us cover from German fighter aircraft and anti-aircraft shells, but others would hinder our mission with turbulence and ice. I can still remember all the names of the different cloud types and how they would affect our flight.

Cirrus cloud formations, that we would see when flying as high as 20,000ft, looked like wisps of smoke and rarely produced any rain.

Stratus is often fairly low-level cloud that forms in flat, generally thick layers. It is associated with overcast dreary days, often with drizzle, but once you climbed through the level of stratus you were often in clear skies above. Stratus hindered finding the target but did make a good hiding place away from Luftwaffe fighters and searchlights.

Cumulus clouds are the puffy, cauliflower type clouds. They are known for turbulence and precipitation, the level depending upon the category of cumulus. Cumulus Nimbus could damage the aircraft, due to severe ice build-up, turbulence and lightening. We tried our best to avoid them, but sometimes we would end up in one without warning or would have to fly through it as we had no other choice.

In amongst all the fear and anticipation there were also many moments of beauty and wonder. I used to love seeing the vortices forming off the aircraft wing tips in certain atmospheric conditions, leaving a white trail behind the aircraft.

We also witnessed some beautiful moments with the clouds shining silver in the moonlight, or witnessed the beauty of the sun setting from altitude.

A schoolboy prayer stayed with me and I would often recite it silently to myself as we flew along or to relax me when I finally returned to my bed in the Nissen hut after combat:

Hello God, I called tonight to talk a little while,

I need a friend who'll listen to my anxiety and my trial.

You see, I can't quite make it through a day just on my own,

I need your love to guide me so I'll never feel alone.

I want to ask you please to keep my family safe and sound

And fill their lives with confidence for whatever fate they're bound.

Give me faith, dear God, to face each hour throughout the day

And not to worry over things I can't change in any way.

I thank you God, for being home and listening to my call,

For giving me such good advice when I stumble and I fall.

Your number, God, is the only one that answers every time.

I never get a busy signal, never had to pay a dime.

So thank you, God, for listening to my troubles and my sorrow.

Good night, God, I love you too and I'll call again tomorrow.

Barbara Ford (now Barbara Meller).   *Gordon Ford.*

Twins Pat and Pam Ford (now Pat Martin and Pam Lunam).

CHAPTER 18

15 SQUADRON AND LOVE AT FIRST SIGHT

During April 1945, we were told that our pilot was about to be promoted to a Squadron Leader and as such, we would now be transferring as a crew to RAF Mildenhall. Whenever we changed base, we always had to total up our flying hours, get them signed off by an officer and then start a new page in our logbook for our new base.

We finally made our transfer to join 15 Squadron on 26th April 1945. Our new squadron emblem was a hind's head (a deer) between wings. This emblem had been chosen due to the squadron originally flying Hawker Hind aircraft. The squadron's motto was "Aim Sure". Both the emblem and motto had been assigned to the squadron by King Edward VIII in May 1936, during his short reign before he abdicated the throne to marry Wallis Simpson.

15 Squadron went from flying Hawker Hind biplanes in 1934 to Bristol Blenheims, followed by Vickers Wellingtons, Short Stirlings and then in 1943 the squadron moved onto Avro Lancasters. Whilst they were still operating Stirlings, 15 Squadron were privileged to be gifted the Stirling bomber named "MacRobert's Reply".

Lady Rachel MacRobert J.P, BSc, GGS, of Douneside, Tarland, Aberdeenshire, Scotland, was the widow of Sir Alexander MacRobert, Baronet of Crawnmore and Cromar, who was the founder of the British India Corporation. Sir Alexander died from a heart attack in 1922 leaving Rachel with three young boys to raise and a large international corporation to run.

Years later, her eldest son, Sir Alasdair MacRobert, became a pilot and in 1937 set up his own small passenger airline called the Indian Aviation Development Company. Tragically, Alasdair was killed on 1st June 1938 when the aircraft he was flying crashed near Luton Airport in Bedfordshire, the cause was not known.

Lady Rachel's second son, Sir Roderic Alan MacRobert, was killed in combat three years later while serving as a pilot with RAF 237 Squadron in the Middle East. He was killed leading a squadron of Hurricanes in an attack on Monsul air base on 22nd May 1941. The attack was a huge success causing considerable damage to the Luftwaffe base and destroying many of the Junkers and Messerschmitts based there, but sadly Roderic did not make it back to base. Her youngest son, Sir Iain Workman MacRobert, was also a very keen aviation enthusiast, so volunteered to join the RAF as a Pilot Officer on 3rd November 1940 and soon after joined the Coastal Command. On receiving the news of Sir Roderic's death, the RAF granted Sir Iain a short period of leave, which he spent with his mother. Approximately five weeks later, on 30th June 1941, Sir Iain himself was reported missing presumed dead, whilst undertaking an air-sea rescue search for a bomber crew known to have ditched into the North Sea. Sir Iain MacRobert has no known grave and is remembered on the RAF Memorial at Runnymede in Surrey.

On 22nd August 1941 Lady MacRobert, wrote a letter to the Secretary of State for Air:

"It is my wish to make a mother's immediate reply in the way that I know would also be my boys' reply; attacking, striking sharply, straight to the mark – the gift of £25,000 – to buy a bomber to carry on their work in the most effective way. This expresses my reaction on receiving the news about my sons … In any case they would be glad that their mother replied for them, and helped to strike a blow at the enemy. So I feel that a suitable name for the bomber would be 'MacRobert's *Reply*'…

If I had ten sons, I know they would all have followed that line of duty. It is with a mother's pride that I enclose a cheque for £25,000 and with it goes my sympathies to those mothers who have also lost their sons, and gratitude to all mothers whose sons so gallantly carry on the fight."

Lady Rachel's Stirling bomber lasted an impressive four months, successfully completing twelve missions in combat between October 1941 and February 1942, before veering off the runway on landing and being written off. After this accident a second Stirling aircraft W7531 was called MacRobert's Reply in order to carry on the name. This aircraft lasted two months in action before being shot down in combat. That was the last aircraft to be named MacRobert's Reply, until 15 Squadron gave the name to a Hawker Siddeley Buccaneer in 1982, in remembrance. Later the name was transferred to a Tornado and was kept part of the squadron's tradition until the squadron was finally disbanded in 2017.

In 1942 Lady MacRobert donated a further £20,000 to the Air Ministry specifically to purchase four Hawker Hurricane fighter aircraft, three of which were named after each of her sons, Sir Roderic, Sir Alasdair and Sir Iain and the fourth was called The Lady. All four Hurricanes were handed over to 94 Squadron in Eygpt, in which Sir Roderic had served. Lady MacRobert also donated a large house in Scotland where members of the Royal Air Force could go for rest and recuperation. Her donations were extremely timely as at this point Great Britain's gold reserves were almost exhausted by the war effort. 15 Squadron had a proud heritage that I was pleased to be part of.

As we settled into our new base at Mildenhall, the war was

definitely still not over, but the newspapers and radio stations were full of optimistic reports that the Nazis were looking close to surrender. Operational flights were becoming few and far between and so our sorties were for training purposes instead of combat. You could feel the mood amongst us all relaxing. On our arrival at Mildenhall, we were given a couple of days off in order to allow our pilot to settle into his new role as Squadron Leader. A couple of days off at short notice, didn't give us enough time to plan trips home, so instead we decided to just have a few lazy days off at the base.

We spent our first day off just relaxing, but by the second day I was feeling restless and bored, so I managed to persuade the rest of the crew to go for a walk and explore the areas surrounding our new base. The main entrance to RAF Mildenhall led out into the pretty village of Beck Row.

It was a beautiful sunny day as we set off through Beck Row and worked our way around the perimeter of the airfield into the village of West Row. As we strolled along, we came to a river, called the River Lark, so we followed the footpath along its banks. This brought us to a lovely country pub called The Ferry Inn. It was a stunning scene - a beautiful stream, with an old, hump-backed, stone bridge crossing over the river.

The river bordered The Ferry Inn gardens and near the river was a young weeping willow tree. Sitting under that tree, enjoying the early spring sunshine, were two young women with their bicycles lying on the ground next to them. It was such a beautiful tranquil sight that I felt drawn to cross the bridge and just be part of this scene. One of our crew, Pete Potter, who was our rear gunner, suggested we go down and have a friendly chat with the women. I couldn't take my eyes off the girl with beautiful long brown hair and hazel eyes. She was so beautiful and I just felt at ease talking to her. She had a lovely gentle, innocent character, yet she conducted herself with such grace and poise. I found out that her name was Barbara, that she lived nearby with her parents and that she had younger twin sisters called Pat and Pam and an older brother called Gerald. The rest of our crew wandered off leaving Pete and I alone to chat with the two girls. It was clear that Pete was equally as captivated by Barbara's friend Pearl.

The girls were very interested to hear about our experiences as aircrew, but in this beautiful location, it was the last thing we wanted to be reminded of, so we talked about everything else instead.

Barbara told us that although she lived so close, she had only been onto the airfield at Mildenhall once, when she was six years old, to watch the start of the England to Australia Air Race, on 20th October 1934. The race was sponsored by Sir Macpherson Robertson, a wealthy businessman who owned a large chocolate factory in Melbourne, Australia. The businessman provided a £15,000 prize for the first aircraft to land in Melbourne. There were compulsory stops at Baghdad, Allahabad, Singapore, Darwin, Charleville and Queensland, before finally arriving at Melbourne. Huge crowds including dignitaries, newspaper journalists and radio presenters were all at Mildenhall airfield to witness the start of the race. Barbara was only young, but remembered the excitement of the day very clearly and could recall seeing the famous female pilot Amy Johnson getting into her aircraft with her husband Jim Mollison. Twenty aircraft took off, but only eleven made it to Melbourne. Sadly, two crew members in a Fairey Fox were killed during the race when their aircraft crashed in Italy. Amy Johnson and her husband Jim Mollison got lost and had to divert to Jabalpur. Sadly, there was no suitable high-octane fuel available at Jabalpur, but rather than quit at this point, they decided to give ordinary petrol a try. They made it to Allahabad, but had to retire at that point as both engines were wrecked from using the wrong fuel.

We all said how sad it was that Amy Johnson had tragically gone missing, presumed shot down, whilst ferrying an aircraft for the war effort in 1941. Amy was part of the Air Transport Auxiliary (ATA) . These pilots ferried new, repaired and damaged military aircraft between factories, air force bases and scrapyards. The ATA employed 1,320 ferry pilots, 168 of which were female. Fifteen of these women lost their lives ferrying aircraft, Amy Johnson being one of them. Not only did these intrepid women act as incredible role models to young women by literally showing that even the sky was no limit, but just as extraordinary, they were granted pay equal to that of their male counterparts, which was ground breaking in the 1940s. These women made a huge contribution to the war effort, but also had a significant impact on the liberation of women.

Pete and I were flying that night, so all too soon we

reluctantly had to drag ourselves away from Barbara and Pearl and set off to catch up with our crew, but every spare moment I had, I found myself thinking about Barbara. I just couldn't get her out of my mind. I suddenly understood what people meant by love at first sight.

The next day as soon as I was able, I went straight back to the weeping willow tree, but sadly there was no sign of Barbara, so I decided to take a stroll around the village in the hope that I might see her, but she was nowhere to be found.

The more I searched the more I realised I couldn't rest until I found her. Finally, out of desperation I stopped an elderly lady walking through the village and quickly made up a story. I told her I had met a very nice man who had asked me to visit him, but I had mislaid his name and address, however I knew that he had twin daughters. The lady's face immediately lit up with recognition and she said: "That can only be Gordon Ford who works at Morley's Garage." She started to explain how to find Morley's, but in the end, I managed to persuade her that I would prefer to see him at his home address instead, so finally she gave me directions to his home. I thanked the lady and set off excitedly. The address she gave me was 2 Pott Hall Road. It was only a short walk, and I immediately knew I'd found the right address, when I saw two identical young girls playing hop-scotch in the middle of the road outside their house. I asked one of the twins to tell their sister Barbara that I would like to see her. The twins, Pat and Pam, ran into the house giggling and came back out with Barbara. She was just as beautiful as I had remembered.

I was needed at base that evening, but made arrangements to meet her the following day. I felt like I was walking on air all the way back to the camp. Seventy-five years later and we're still together with seventy-one years of happy marriage behind us, and two wonderful grown up children, two granddaughters and three great grandchildren.

I will never forget that first meeting with Barbara, under the weeping willow tree. Every time we saw each other I knew I was in love, but Barbara was only seventeen and I was only twenty. Barbara was too young to sign up to help with the war effort, but had still seen first-hand a few of the horrors of war.

When she was only 13 years old, she had witnessed a Wellington bomber shot down by a Nazi fighter aircraft. The Wellington had finished its mission and was just coming in to land at RAF Mildenhall when it was attacked by a German fighter aircraft. The Wellington caught fire and crashed on top of a cottage in Beck Row with the tragic loss of all of its crew members. Thankfully, the owners of the cottage, Mr and Mrs Titmarsh, escaped unhurt. They had taken refuge under their bed on hearing gunfire and although the cottage was pretty much flattened their bedroom was left intact. The Titmarshes were a lovely couple and Mr Titmarsh ran an insurance agency in the village. It was the first major incident in the village and everyone found it really upsetting.

Some time later another Wellington bomber was so badly

damaged after returning from a raid that its undercarriage collapsed on landing. The aircraft overshot the runway and skidded into a barley field at the edge of a smallholding belonging to Mr Norman, very close to Barbara's house.

On 1st September 1941, a Wellington bomber from 99 Squadron, had finished its raid on Cologne, but had insufficient fuel to return to its base at Brize Norton, so was in the process of diverting to RAF Mildenhall. The approach profile was all wrong, perhaps because the pilot was unfamiliar with Mildenhall or maybe due to damage to the aircraft and its handling. The pilot had to make a go around after his first approach and sadly was shot down by an enemy fighter as he made his second approach. The aircraft crashed into a field in West Row village, right next to Barbara's house. People from the village all rushed to the scene, but only the rear gunner survived. The wreckage was finally removed, but for a few weeks it remained in the field as a sad monument to its crew, reminding everyone who saw it of the risks being taken daily by our airmen.

Even though it was clear that the war was coming to an end, we still had to keep up with our training flights and never knew when we went in for our briefing whether we might be expected to go into combat that night or not. I had no way to communicate with Barbara, as like most households, her family didn't have a telephone. Barbara just had to wait until I arrived unannounced at her door. Barbara's house was on the approach path to the runway so she could clearly see the aircraft coming in to land from the window at the top of her stairs. She and I devised a plan that I would ask my pilot to flash the landing light on and off and dip his wings as we came in to land so that she would know it was me. Every time Barbara heard an aircraft coming in to land, she would rush upstairs, sit on her landing floor and look out of the window, waiting and hoping to see a landing light flashing on and off as it flew over her house.

I had only known her a short time, but I now literally lived for the moments when I would turn up at Barbara's house. It didn't matter where we went, it was just wonderful to be in her company.

Cis and Alf's wedding day.

My sister's American husband, Alf, and myself.

My parents, Ada and Herbert Meller.

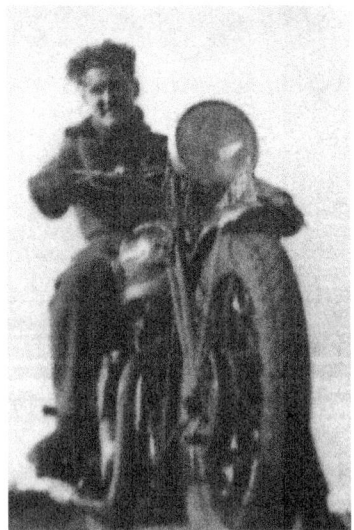

Pete's motorbike.

My MG sports car, one of the early T-Series.

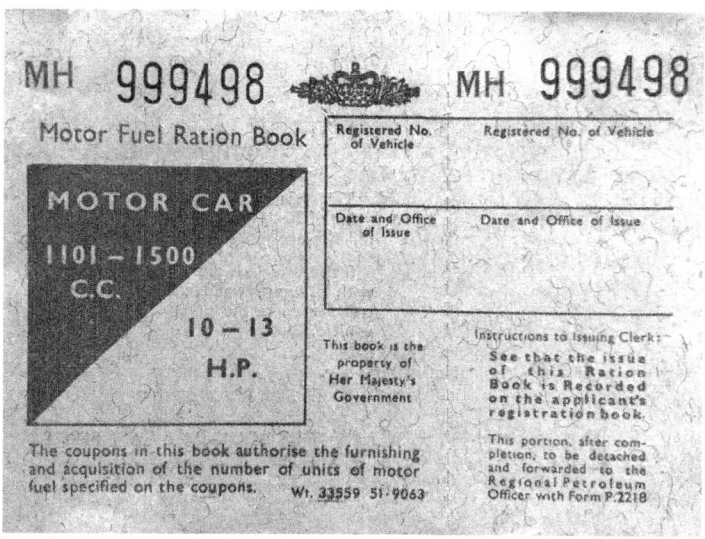

A fuel ration book cover.

CHAPTER 19

MY MG

Not long after I met Barbara, I took a trip home to Warrington for my sister's wedding. Cissie was getting married to an American serviceman, Alf Cotnoir, who I'd met once briefly on a visit home. He was a USAAF chef at the US base at Burtonwood and a most likeable person. I was thrilled to receive a letter from home that included my wedding invitation card. As excited as I was, I realised that there was very little chance of me being able to attend, but by some small miracle, those precious days off were granted to me.

In my package from home, was a box of chocolates, a five-pound note and a lengthy letter from my mother, which I took back to my Nissen hut to enjoy.

I was troubled to read that my younger brother Herbert

had been injured. He had been sent home from the front line on convalescent leave, having had a skin graft. My mother explained that they had taken skin from his thigh to cover an injury to his right arm, which had been caused by shrapnel. Apparently, his regiment had at first been on the offensive, then had pulled back to allow the enemy to advance, before making a pincer movement, surrounding them. My brother had been badly injured by shrapnel and was lying semi-conscious amongst other soldiers, who were either dead or dying. German tanks were fast approaching. Some of Herbert's comrades had found a small amount of refuge in a ditch and were huddled down hoping that the tanks wouldn't see them, when they saw Herbert groaning and moving in pain. They risked their own lives, leaving the safety of their ditch, to rush out, grab him and drag him back. Seconds later, the Panzers rumbled by and those in the ditch had the harrowing experience of listening to the heart-rending screams - both German and English, as the tanks ploughed over injured bodies. I just couldn't begin to imagine what Herbert and all his colleagues were suffering and experiencing. As delighted as I was to hear that he had survived with this narrow escape, I was extremely saddened to read further down in the letter, that he had already been signed off as fit and was now back on the front line in Germany again. I sat there staring at the letter with great sadness and said a prayer for my brother's safety.

The occasion of my sister's wedding soon arrived and it was wonderful to see my family and friends again. It was such light relief from all the pressures of war, a wonderfully happy and uplifting celebration. Sadly, my brother wasn't able to be there, as he was still fighting out in Germany and we had no way of contacting him. We all missed his company, as he was always fun to be around especially at parties. It was interesting hearing all about the changes at Burtonwood airfield now that it was under US management. So much had happened to that strip of land since the days when my sister, brother and I had been stranded out there in the middle of a thunderstorm. I wondered what had happened to the lovely lady who had taken us in on that day and to her charming house.

I had only been allocated a few days leave for Cissie's wedding and it had taken me a lot longer than I had hoped to travel home, as the train service and other forms of public transport were at best erratic or non-existent. I wanted to stay as long as I possibly could, to enjoy the moment with my family, so one of my old school friends, Jack Casey, suggested I buy a car for the journey back to base. He knew a local car sales firm and took me over to buy one. I chose an Austin T saloon that cost me £2.00 and included some petrol coupons to get me home. I'd never driven a car before, so Jack showed me how and explained how to start it and how to deal with the more common issues of keeping a car on the road. I learned how to double clutch, change gear, pull out the choke to get it to start and how to steer. Jack came with me for a test drive around Warrington, to help me get used to it before I set off on my journey back to Norfolk.

It was a long journey with me struggling to get to grips with changing gear without stalling, but I soon got the hang of it. Thankfully, the roads were very quiet, due to the fact that there had been very few, if any, private vehicles manufactured during the war, and petrol was still rationed. Jack had warned me to be careful when driving through towns where there were trams, as people were so preoccupied with catching the tram, they forgot to look out for any other traffic and would just dash out in front of you. He also told me to avoid getting my wheels stuck in the tramlines. Electric trams were a very popular form of public transport during this period, as they were cheap to run and low in pollution. I had noticed that I could see the road below me through a few gaps in the Austin's floor, so I doubted that my vehicle would cope very well with being knocked about on tramlines. Despite the obvious issues with my vehicle, I was still completely delighted to own my first ever car.

There were no motorways in Great Britain at the time and the route I took was not the easiest, but I deliberately chose it because I knew the scenery through the Peak District would be spectacular. I just wanted to savour the moment of having my own car and being free to drive any route I chose. I might have chosen the best route for the scenery, but definitely chose the wrong route for my poor old Austin T saloon. I can remember admiring one of the most stunning areas of the Peak District, ascending a particularly steep section of the road, with just a narrow grass verge protecting my car and me from a deep ravine, when my car started to struggle. As we neared the top, it suddenly became clear that the struggle had got the better of the engine. Even though my foot was flat to the floor and it was in first gear, the car could no longer make the climb and started to roll backwards down the road. I used both my foot break and the hand brake, but it still didn't bring the car to a halt. Thankfully, a well-positioned signpost, warning road users to be careful not to drop into the ravine, stopped my vehicle as I slid back down the hill and bumped into it. I could not believe my incredible good fortune, as after everything I had been through, I really didn't want to die plummeting into a ravine in a runaway car.

I spent a considerable time checking the engine over and then trying to drive, before finally deciding it was best to abandon the car and start walking. I had not seen another vehicle or person along this route, so there was no one to ask for help. I had just satisfied myself that I had retrieved all my personal possessions and was closing the car door when a large saloon car drove past, stopped and reversed. I noticed that there was an official pennant on the bonnet. As the car stopped opposite mine, an army officer leaned out of the rear window and asked me what the trouble was. I explained as quickly as I could and added that I urgently had to get back to RAF Mildenhall by midnight. The officer then spoke to his chauffeur who got into my car and started the engine. It started straight away and the driver looked at me as if to say, "there is nothing wrong with this car", until he put it into gear and tried to drive it. Having concluded that my vehicle was beyond roadside repair, the officer took control of the situation. He instructed me to stay with my car while his driver drove him to the nearby town of Buxton, where he knew there was a garage. He told me he would then send the driver back with a towrope to rescue me.

I sat patiently in my car and waited and hoped that they wouldn't forget about me, but true to his word the driver returned with a towrope. While we attached the towrope, the driver explained that the army officer was a Lieutenant General and one of the nicest people you could ever wish to meet. With the towrope in place, my Austin and I precariously made our way into Buxton with me sweating with concentration, determined not to roll into the back of the stately army car. I didn't get to see the officer again as the driver had taken him to his destination first before rescuing me, so I asked the driver to thank him for me. I thanked the driver profusely for rescuing me and offered him a ten-shilling note, which he politely refused, before wishing me good luck and driving away.

The proprietor of the garage informed me that the officer had offered to pay for the loan of the towrope and had instructed him to do whatever he could to get me on the road again. The engineer spent a while looking over my vehicle and then returned with the unwelcome news that my engine would have to be re-bored or a new engine fitted, which obviously I didn't have time for. So instead he offered to part exchange the Austin for a two-seated MG sports car that was sitting on his forecourt for sale. I quite literally emptied my pockets and I only had a few pound notes that my mother had slipped into my pocket and the ten-shilling note that I had offered as a thank you to the driver. I was a bit overwhelmed and shocked when the garage owner accepted this meagre payment, helped me transfer my belongings into the MG and sent me off on my way.

I couldn't believe my luck, the MG sports car was in a totally different league to the Austin and I absolutely loved it. You should have seen all my friends' faces when I finally arrived back at base that evening, in my beautiful little sports car. It was so low to the ground that the security guard at the gate didn't even have to raise the barrier, I just drove straight under it. The next morning everyone wanted a turn at driving it and some of the RAF engineers offered to keep it serviced for me, as they just wanted the opportunity to work on it. It required very little maintenance - just the spark plugs to be cleaned and a regular oil and filter change. There were no indicators, you just stuck your hand out to show which way you were turning, but really there was so little traffic on the roads it hardly mattered. That little car brought so much excitement back to base with it and we were all extremely grateful to have such a fun distraction. What an incredible gift that garage owner gave us.

I couldn't wait to drive my new car to pick up Barbara. I can still remember her face when I pulled up outside her house. We had some wonderful moments driving around in this beautiful little red sports car; people would wave to us as we drove past. On one occasion, Pete, our rear gunner, asked if he could borrow my car as he wanted to take his girlfriend shopping in

Bury St Edmunds. As I had already promised to take Barbara to Mildenhall, I agreed he could borrow the car if I could borrow his motorcycle, although I had never ridden one before. Under Pete's instructions, I drove his motorcycle round the perimeter of the airfield, ending up in a ditch before picking Barbara up. It was definitely an eventful journey and I was far from safe, with no form of safety gear or crash helmets and the road to Mildenhall was extremely undulating. I can't believe now that I risked Barbara's safety, due to the folly of youth. Thankfully, we survived our journey unharmed, but I have never ridden a motorcycle since.

Barbara always jokes that she had some of her most hair-raising experiences along that particular country lane. When she was sixteen, she was cycling home on her own after leaving Mildenhall cinema where she worked part time as an usherette. It was a really dark night and her bicycle light was partly shaded due to the wartime regulations, so was providing very little illumination. She was concentrating hard on keeping to the road when she heard a faint sound that frightened her coming from the hedge. She glanced briefly over her shoulder and all she could see in the darkness was a ghostly white shape floating over the hedgerow and following her. It scared her half to death, so she pedalled for all she was worth, gasping for breath. She didn't slow down until reaching the crossroads not far from her home, when the white shape finally overtook her and flew off into the darkness and disappeared. Still spooked, Barbara powered home, threw her cycle on the ground outside her front door and bolted into her house. After he finished laughing, her father explained that it would simply have been a barn owl out looking for prey.

CHAPTER 20

VICTORY IN EUROPE

O n 16th April 1945 the Russian Red Army entered Berlin. For four years they had pushed the German army out of Soviet Russia, across Poland and back into Eastern Germany.

Mussolini and his partner Clara Petacci, knew that German rule was now in tatters and decided that the time had come to flee Italy, so they set off in a convoy with other Nazi sympathisers, heading for the safety of Switzerland. As they tried to cross the border Italian partisans recognised them and had them all executed. Their bodies were then dumped in Milan's Piazzale Loreto. Clara and Mussolini's bodies were tied up by their ankles and left dangling in the centre of the square. This was deeply symbolic, as only eight months earlier Hitler had ordered a similar fate to fifteen Italian partisans.

With the Russian Red Army now in Berlin, Hitler knew it was only a matter of days before he needed to surrender. It is thought that Mussolini's fate played heavily on Hitler's mind and he must have been worried that the same fate awaited him and his girlfriend Eva Braun.

On 30th April 1945, Nazi leader Adolf Hitler committed suicide, although this wasn't confirmed until a few days later, on 2nd May, when the Soviet Russian army accepted the surrender of what little remained of Hitler's army.

Hitler and Eva Braun poisoned themselves by each taking a cyanide capsule. Hitler first poisoned his pet dog, a wolfhound named Blondi, to test the strength of the cyanide capsule. Hitler left orders that their bodies should be burned in the Chancellery garden. The following day, Joseph Goebbels, the Reich Minister of Propaganda, and his wife Magda decided to take their own lives and those of their young children too. They arranged for a dentist, Helmet Kunz, to inject their six children with a high dose of morphine so that they were unconscious, Magda then placed a crushed cyanide tablet into each of their mouths, before she and Goebbels took a cyanide capsule themselves.

The day before Hitler committed suicide, Lancaster bombers started Operation Manna. British intelligence had informed our government of a humanitarian crisis in the Netherlands where over 20,000 people had already starved to death and the majority of the remaining population would not live much longer unless they received food. People were surviving by eating anything that could be deemed edible, such as flower bulbs, rotten food, animal food and even pets, continually boiling the same old bones in order to try to obtain some tiny amount of nutrients.

To weaken resistance, the Nazis had a policy of stopping local food production and removing produce from occupied areas, leaving civilians struggling for food and in no fit state to consider rebellion. The Netherlands had literally been stripped of food and its 3.5 million civilians had been left to starve to death. The Dutch were unable to import food as all the railway lines had been bombed. The quickest way to get food to these poor people was to fly our bombers with their bomb bays full of food, as low as possible over the region, in the hope of reaching as many people as possible. It was named Operation Manna, after the Biblical miracle of God dropping manna from heaven to sustain the Israelites.

The German Commander-in-Chief, General Johannes Blaskowitz sanctioned the specified drop zones and agreed to a ceasefire.

Two Lancasters made a test flight on 29th April, each aircraft dropping their cargo of food in five special panniers. Each pannier contained seventy sacks of food. The panniers had to be tough as they were not equipped with parachutes, so the aircraft had to make their drops as low as practically possible to reduce the damage. Both aircraft returned to base without incident. This test flight had been named "Bad Penny" as in the expression "A *bad penny always turns up*".

With the test flight complete, Lancaster aircraft from Groups 1, 3 and 8 flew over 3,000 sorties dropping food supplies. The USA initiated a similar campaign called Operation Chowhound and completed over 2,000 sorties of food drops. Apparently, some aircrew used the Window parachutes and tied small bundles of their own sweets and chocolate to them and dropped them over villages with a message inside reading "*Voor de kinderen*" (for the children).

On 7th May the German High Command Chief of Staff, General Alfred Jodl signed an unconditional surrender of all German Forces at the Allied War Headquarters in Reims, France.

I woke up on the morning of Friday 8th May 1945, to a base buzzing with excitement. We all knew that victory in Europe was imminent, but it was still exciting to hear that the war in Europe was now officially over. One of our crew had a newspaper so we all sat down to read the front page; it stated that Churchill would make an official announcement at 3pm that afternoon. The headlines read: "Wait For It - Til *3 - the war has now ended*". The newspaper headlines across the world were not only covering this story, but were also full of alleged reports of how large numbers of Nazi senior officers were using U-boats to escape to neutral countries such as Brazil, Paraguay and Argentina. The First Lady of Argentina, Eva Peron was named as someone offering refuge to Nazi leaders.

As exciting as it was to hear that the war in Europe was

officially over, we also felt a fairly stoic response to the official Victory in Europe (VE) Day celebrations, as our crew had recently been told that we would soon be deployed overseas to help in the war against the Japanese. World War 2 might have ended in Europe, but it was still raging out in the Pacific.

Later that day I was able to leave base to visit Barbara and her family. At 3pm we all settled down in their front room to listen to the Prime Minister's VE Day speech on the radio:

"My dear friends, this is your hour… This is a victory of the great British nation as a whole. We were the first, in this ancient island, to draw the sword against tyranny. After a while we were left all alone against the most tremendous military power that has been seen. We were all alone for a whole year. There we stood, alone … the lights went out and the bombs came down …

I say that in the long years to come not only will the people of this island but of the world, wherever the bird of freedom chirps in human hearts, look back to what we've done and they will say 'Do not despair, do not yield to violence and tyranny, march straightforward and die if need be – unconquered' …

We must begin the task of rebuilding our hearth and homes, doing our utmost to make this country a land in which all have a chance."

The radio broadcaster announced that there was great jubilation throughout Great Britain, the Commonwealth and all Allied countries around the world. Crowds of people gathered in towns and cities waving flags, linking arms with strangers as they marched along the streets singing well known songs such as: *Roll out the Barrel, Tipperary, Loch Lomond. Bless them all, Pack up your troubles* and in London the popular song: *"I'm going to get lit up when the lights go on in London".* Apparently, in London there were large crowds outside Buckingham Palace and right up the Mall to Admiralty Arch. There were similar scenes of jubilation in city centres everywhere. Everyone just wanted to be out on the streets celebrating and sharing their mutual relief. The broadcaster stated that many bonfires had been lit, in way of celebration, as people had been deprived of light for so long by the black out that any form of light was uplifting and felt like a demonstration of festivity and freedom. One of the things I remember most about VE Day, was hearing the church bells being chimed for the first time in six years. It was such a joyful uplifting sound, which had a certain majesty to it.

At 9pm, King George VI, along with Winston Churchill, the Queen (Queen Elizabeth the Queen Mother), Princess Elizabeth (who is now our current Queen) and her younger sister Princess Margaret all made an appearance on the balcony of Buckingham Palace. After this the two princesses were allowed to sneak out of the Palace in disguise and join in with the celebrations. There were special services of Thanksgiving at a number of churches throughout Great Britain, which had pews full of those wishing to say a prayer of gratitude that right had finally prevailed over might and that light was now restored to Europe.

Victory in Europe was something none of us had dared to dream of throughout the majority of the war. It had seemed like an impossible fight. At one stage the Nazis controlled most of Europe, but incredibly here we were celebrating our victory and with it Europe's freedom. The only way Europe could have been rescued from this tyranny was by the combined force of the Allies; 16 million US personnel, 30 million Soviet Russian troops and over 15 million men and women from all over the Commonwealth around the globe joined in the fight to release Europe from Hitler's rule. To do this the Allies required a base in striking distance of Germany, which Great Britain could provide. Great Britain had done an incredible job holding back the Nazis and preventing them from invading. Our modern world could have been a very different place if the British had been defeated in the Battle of Britain. Of this Churchill said:

> *"Never in the field of human conflict has so much been owed by so many to so few."*

Later that evening, on VE Day, Churchill addressed the celebratory crowds in London. The crowds cheered and clapped and called his name, then sang *For he's a Jolly Good Fellow* and *Land of Hope and Glory.*

Winston Churchill was heralded as a national hero, and lovingly referred to as our very own British bulldog. He delivered some incredibly moving speeches in praise of the British public and all their servicemen. Of Bomber Command he said:

"Night after night, undeterred by the fury of guns and new inventions of death they battled their way across Europe and paid a terrible price."

His amazing powers as a great orator rallied the nation and held them strong. Many years later, at his 80th birthday celebrations, when Churchill was once again being praised for his rousing war speeches, he responded with these words:

"It was the nation and race dwelling all around the globe that had the lion heart. I just had the luck to be called upon to give the roar."

There was no general stand-down for 15 Squadron at RAF Mildenhall, with no VE Day celebrations, just a general feeling of relief that at least this part of the war was ended.

Our squadron's focus was now on the Far East, so we were kept busy with briefings to bring us up-to date with the war against Japan, which was still a very big threat. It was strange because the newspapers and the radio stations were forever stating "now that the war is over", yet for us and thousands of service personnel it most definitely was far from over.

The USA had a huge presence in the Pacific fighting against Japan, but the British 14th Army and our British Pacific Naval Fleet, based in Australia, were out there too. The wartime censor of the media, meant that the war in the Far East, was given minimal press time, so many people didn't even realise that we were still fighting and the 14th Army became known as the "forgotten army".

Whilst Great Britain was busy defending its own soil against Hitler, the Japanese had invaded the British colonies of Malaysia and Singapore in 1941 and then started their invasion of Burma in 1942. The British armed forces in these regions had out of date, inferior equipment. For instance, their air force was equipped with aircraft such as the Brewster Buffalo, an aircraft I had worked on when I was stationed at the Burtonwood Repair Depot. I had been told then, that they would soon be phased out as they were not suitable for effective modern combat.

In 1942 General William Slim (affectionately nicknamed Uncle Bill) was sent out to Burma to try to rally what remained of the Burmese Army and build a fighting force from there. Under his leadership the 14th Army soon became a tremendous fighting force of volunteers from all over the Commonwealth and the Far East, with battalions of Gurkha and Indian troops. In the end this formidable army pushed the Japanese out of Burma and secured it as an Allied stronghold by March 1945.

As the Battle for Europe was nearing completion the Allies turned their attention to securing Okinawa Island in the Pacific as a suitable base within striking distance of Japan. Okinawa was a long, narrow island, 70 miles long and only averaging seven miles wide, of mainly dense sub-tropical foliage, with long white sandy beaches and mountain ridges.

We were briefed that we would shortly be flying out to Okinawa. The only thing delaying our departure was that we were waiting for the delivery of the new Avro Lincoln bombers. These were basically a long-range variant of the Lancaster bomber as we needed the extra fuel capacity for combat sorties over the Pacific.

The island of Okinawa had only been under Allied occupation since April. The battle to gain it was one of the last major battles of World War 2, and the casualty rate was extremely high. The film *Hacksaw Ridge* graphically depicts the horrors of this battle. On 1st April 1945, the Navy's 5th Fleet and more than 180,000 US Army and US Marine Corps troops set foot on the beaches of Okinawa. The Japanese knew that if the Allies could secure Okinawa and its airports then from there they could invade Japan. To finally take control of this crucial island, the Allies had to climb a 400ft escarpment and then battle face to face with the Japanese soldiers waiting for them at the top of their climb. 12,520 US soldiers, 110,000 Japanese soldiers and approximately 150,000 Japanese civilians lost their lives in this terrible battle. Most people in Britain thought the war was over after the celebrations of VE Day, yet World War 2 was still very much a reality for those involved in the battle for Okinawa.

As much as I wanted the war to be over for me too, I was also quite excited at the chance of flying out to Asia and the Pacific. As a child I had no anticipation of leaving Warrington let alone flying half way round the world.

Whilst I was contemplating world travel, my sister was also planning for an epic journey too. Not long after VE Day, I received a letter from home explaining that my sister, Cis, was busy packing for her new life in the USA. Most of the US Armed Forces were being recalled to the USA to restructure their war effort against Japan. This included my new brother-in-law Alf Cotnoir. All English brides, including my sister, were booked to travel over by sea, where they would meet up with their husbands a while later. Over two million US servicemen passed through Great Britain during World War 2 and many married a British bride, who then emigrated with their husbands in 1945.

It must have been exciting, but also daunting for Cis, to be making such an incredible voyage without her family or even her new husband by her side. I was sad that I didn't get the chance to see my sister before her sailing. We had been so close throughout our childhood; I just couldn't imagine her living so far away with the Atlantic Ocean between us. My mother was incredibly sad; it must have been a big wrench for her, but at least both her sons had so far survived the war.

CHAPTER 21

OPERATION EXODUS

I n between training for warfare in the Pacific we were kept very busy as part of Operation Exodus. It was a great honour and privilege to be part of the rescue team sent to repatriate our Prisoners of War (POW). Operation Exodus commenced on 2nd May 1945, as soon as Berlin surrendered to the Russians, but our squadron was not deployed as part of the operation until 12th May 1945. The airport we were sent to was Juvincourt, near Rheims in Northern France. Juvincourt had been a French air force base before Germany invaded. The Nazis then expanded the runway and used it as one of their main operational Luftwaffe bases in France from 1940 until 1944. It was a base for both German fighters and their bomber squadrons. The airfield was seized by our allies during

September 1944 and became a major USAAF base, used for fighter and bomber aircraft as well as a base for transport units to fly in supplies for the remainder of the war.

On our first visit to Juvincourt, we were all taken aback by what we saw. I don't know how many POWs we were expecting, but the rescue mission had already been going on for just over a week, so we were shocked to see this massive airfield still packed solid. The POWs were all just sitting, patiently waiting to be transported home. I was not impressed with the large number of armed Soviet Russian guards who patrolled the airfield, and who were heavily involved in the organisation. I remember being so frustrated by the length of time they were taking to complete the simple task of allocating twenty-four POWs to each aircraft, and sending them on their way. How difficult could that be? Aircraft that had landed a long time before us were still waiting to be loaded. I had to be content to bite my tongue and wait patiently in line with all the others. It was a long wait, but a wonderful feeling when we were finally able to welcome our allocated POWs on board.

We had no passenger seats; POWs had to be given a space to sit along the length of both sides of the fuselage and we had to instruct them to remain in their space throughout the duration of the flight. This procedure was introduced after Lancaster aircraft RF230 crashed, on 9th May, horrifically killing everyone on board. It had been explained to us that the enquiry into the accident suspected that it had been caused by the POWs all moving to the back of the aircraft. This would be like everyone moving to one side of a seesaw, making the aircraft so tail heavy that the pilot would not have been able to push the nose of the aircraft down sufficiently to maintain flight. The aircraft was returning to Britain with twenty-four POWs, some of whom had been incarcerated for over five years. The aircraft entered a spin from which it could not recover and it crashed, killing everyone on board. We were all greatly affected by this horrific accident. All crews were subsequently advised to brief the POWs about the importance of remaining in their allocated position throughout the flight.

As our passengers boarded, it was upsetting to see the sorry, unkempt state they were all in. They were all noticeably underweight, but the greatest sadness was the blank look in their eyes and the fact that they didn't seem to feel that they could make eye contact with us. They just filed quietly on board. It was clear that even as they boarded a British aircraft on their way home, they still felt like POWs; a state of mind that the Russian guards at the airport were still enforcing. However, once airborne I think they finally allowed themselves to believe that their ordeal was over and freedom was beginning to dawn. By the time we landed and we were helping them off, you could already see a significant change in their demeanour, and smiles emerging. On landing there were vehicles waiting to transport them to one of the transit camps where they would soon be issued with new clothing as well as being given a full medical examination and their first decent meal for years.

Due to the long delay being experienced in Juvincourt, on

one occasion we had to stay overnight and sleep in the aircraft. Even though it was May, it was very cold that night, therefore to help us keep warm we pulled the ripcords on our parachutes and covered ourselves with the fabric, but we were still all moaning about being cold. We figured that we couldn't use the parachutes on our return journey anyway as we would not be able to bail out and leave the passengers on board. We could not help but feel for these POWs, waiting patiently to be released by the Soviet Russian troops. It wasn't even a comfortable flight home for them, with their backs pressed up against the metal fuselage of the Lancaster. Even in May it was cold at altitude in the back of a bomber and they didn't have our flight suits to keep them warm. We had to keep below 10,000ft with passengers on board as we only had enough oxygen masks for the crew. The noise, the cold and the discomfort took it out of the POWs, but you could see in their eyes their relief to be back on British soil and finally released from the oppression of guards.

Whilst waiting in line each time in Juvincourt, I would find myself scanning the men sitting waiting, always in the desperate hope that I would see someone I knew who had been missing presumed dead. Sadly, I never did see anyone I recognised.

On one of our flights back from Juvincourt we were informed that we would be carrying Group Captain Batchelor back to base as a positioning flight. He sat up front with our captain for the flight home.

On another trip, on 15th May, I was busy helping some of the POW passengers on board our aircraft, when I looked up and saw one of the passengers hobbling towards the Lancaster, with tears of relief and recognition streaming down his face. None of our crew knew him as he'd been a POW for a long while, but he recognised the letters "LS" on the side of the aircraft as belonging to his own squadron. We may not have known him directly, but it felt like welcoming a long lost member of your family on board.

Due to the large number of POWs, this method of repatriation continued until the end of June 1945. It must have been hard waiting your turn, particularly if you were one of the last, having to wait six weeks, desperate to return home to loved ones, still stuck in that classification of being a POW, still feeling very much oppressed, even though technically now free.

Having completed our trips out to Juvincourt, there wasn't an immediate role for us so it was decided to send most of our squadron, particularly those who had been on operations, out on a "Rest Camp" for a week. It was early June in 1945 and the weather was wonderful. We were sent by transport down to East Runton, a lovely location on the north Norfolk coast. It was interesting sitting in the back of our RAF transport lorry watching the countryside going by. People in the country had been far better off during the war, as most had been able to use their gardens to supplement their diets. Most people had a large vegetable patch and were rearing animals such as chickens, rabbits, a goat, a pig or even a cow. None of their food was ever wasted; most people bartered or traded rather than paid cash for things. We passed a sign saying "freshly caught wild rabbit for sale". A number of people living in the country would catch wild animals such as rabbits, hares and pheasants, while others would catch fish from the local rivers.

It was also very noticeable how much our lifestyle was changing from when I was born in 1924. Women were now wearing trousers, going into church without wearing a hat, flying aircraft, driving cars, vans and lorries. Our eating habits had also changed. We were now eating unpeeled potatoes and a variety of peas we didn't have to shell, in order to utilise every scrap and minimise wastage. Anything not edible for human consumption went to your pig or a friend's pig or goat.

When we arrived at the campsite, there were eight RAF tents set in one corner of the field on a small clifftop, not far from the beach and only a short walk from the village. There were several other private tents at the other end of the campsite. We were told to give the families some privacy, so we stuck to our half of the field. I was told that I was in charge and that everyone must report to me and then we were left alone to get on with it. With only a small amount of organisation it was amazing how everyone soon fitted in doing the necessary jobs. One of my friends offered to do all the cooking; before the war he had been a manager of a pie factory in the Midlands, so we felt that this qualified him as the camp chef! He did a tremendous job on the barbecue and made us some fantastic meals. He even arranged with some local fishermen to bring us their daily catch. It was remarkable how organised we were in a very short time. I just remember it as being a thoroughly relaxing week.

I had taken my boxing gloves and a boxer's punch ball with me and used this leisure time to get back into boxing training again. It was a great therapy, taking my mind off all the horrors of war. The beach defences had been removed and we were able to go swimming in the sea, but the best thing was just the freedom to do as we pleased when we pleased. Most of us would stay up late at night, just chatting. It was strange but liberating to be able to discuss such matters as the economy, politics, our favourite comedians, sports and the latest news topics.

One major topic of conversation was the forthcoming general election and whom we would be voting for. There could have been no better wartime leader than our Prime Minister Winston Churchill, but Britain had been completely bankrupted through our war effort, so now it had to be decided whether Churchill was the best man to lead our country back towards some sort of solvency. Winston Churchill wanted to keep the coalition government going until the end of the war against Japan, but Clement Attlee, the Labour leader, insisted upon an election. On 23rd May 1945 the coalition government was dissolved and Winston Churchill was asked to form a caretaker government to rule over the country until an election date could be organised.

Another major topic of conversation was what would happen to Lord Haw-Haw. His real name was William Brooke Joyce, but he was nicknamed Lord Haw-Haw because of the haughty affected English accent he used when broadcasting pro-Nazi propaganda on the radio throughout the war. His broadcasts

Rest Camp at East Runton, on the Norfolk coast.

Raising the RAF flag at East Runton.

Sparring at Rest Camp.

Representing RAF Bomber Command as a Middleweight boxer.

would start with the phrase "Germany Calling". Joyce soon became the most hated man in Great Britain, after Hitler. He and his wife emigrated to Germany at the outbreak of war and soon set up a small radio station in Hamburg sending English language propaganda broadcasts by medium wave radio. People in the Great Britain would accidently pick up the station whilst tuning in their radios. It is difficult to explain the impact it had on you when tuning in your radio to come across a very affected English accent delivering German propaganda into your household. You just somehow felt violated by him. After the war Joyce was captured and there was much speculation as to what would happen to him. It wasn't until 17th September 1945 that Joyce finally went on trial, was found guilty of treason and was sentenced to death. He was hanged on 3rd January 1946, making him the last man to ever be hanged for treason in Great Britain, before the death penalty was finally abolished in 1969.

Another top subject that we discussed at great length was the fact that the government was discussing getting rid of Double British Summer Time. Who knows why the decision was made, but most people thought that this was a backward step and I still believe our country would benefit by going back to Double British Summer Time.

We all had a wonderful week away in East Runton and felt thoroughly rejuvenated when we returned to base. However, our mood was diminished somewhat on our arrival as there was an auction in progress, selling off all the abandoned vehicles left by crews who had lost their lives. It was shocking just how many vehicles there were. The auction was being held to raise funds for the families of those who had died. There were numerous motorcars, motorcycles and bicycles. The majority of cars and motorbikes were purchased by trades people, as they mostly required a lot of maintenance to get them roadworthy again as many had been parked up for a long time. Most cars sold for less money than the bicycles, as the cost of maintenance, plus fuel rationing, meant that most people could not afford to run a car, thereby making bicycles in much greater demand and therefore worth more money.

A few days after this auction I visited a breakers yard with our rear gunner Pete who wanted a part for his motorcycle. On looking round the yard I saw, perched on the bonnet of a wrecked car, a brass angel ornament. Something about it just attracted me to it, and I didn't like to see it sitting there amongst all the wreckage. The yard owner dismantled it from the bonnet of the car and sold it to me for a few pence. I have no idea what type of car it was for, but I just liked it as an ornament and still have it to this day. Maybe it was just that the angel reminded me of my childhood near death experience. Strange how I'd come so close to heaven's gate back then, but somehow had managed to survive the battle of Europe. Now I just had to survive my next big campaign which had been code-named Operation Tiger Force.

CHAPTER 22

TOURING EUROPE

After our Rest Camp, it was back to work flying sorties over Germany, but this time we were focusing a camera lens, not our bombsights. We nicknamed these sorties "Cooks Tours" after the holiday company Thomas Cook. On occasions, we were allowed to take members of the ground crew with us, who had worked incredibly hard throughout the war to keep our Lancasters airborne. The first trip we made we had Air Commodore Kirkpatrick OBE as our pilot. The planned route took us over Wesel, Osnabruck, Bremen, Hamburg, Hannover, Bielefeld Viaduct, Hamm, Kamen, Essen, Duisburg and Dortmund all in Germany and then Westkappelle in the Netherlands on our return flight. The purpose of these flights was to assess damage and collect photographic records.

It was strange to finally get a proper look at these destinations in Europe, but it would have been far more satisfying to have seen them in their former glory, rather than the sorry state these cities and their occupants were now in following the mass destruction caused by World War 2.

As part of our tour of Europe, we landed in Hamburg, the largest city in Germany after Berlin. We were provided with some transport to take us into the city centre. It was incredibly sad to see the damage our bombs had caused. It seemed that about 75% of the city had been completely turned to rubble. Most of the inhabitants appeared to be women and children living in the cellars of bombed out houses. Access to their cellars was formed by dug out trenches through a huge pile of debris that had once been their home. There were no gardens just piles upon piles of wreckage everywhere. You couldn't help but marvel at the invincible spirit of children who had immediately turned the havoc of this metropolis into a play area. Many of the children had bare feet and were playing a game whereby they picked up bits of rubble with their toes, seeing who could pitch the debris the furthest. Others threw stones at bottles in competition, whilst a group played hide and seek. Their clothes were ragged and they were all underweight, but it was good to see that the spirit of childhood still prevailed.

The city was pretty much flattened in every direction as far as the eye could see. The few remaining buildings were being occupied by Allied troops. It was sad, but we were seen as the occupying, invading force, and as such, as we approached any of the city's inhabitants, even children, they would immediately get out of our way, vacating the footpath to let us through and would look down avoiding eye contact. They quite literally looked defeated and it was very sad to witness and to feel that we were seen as the cause. Ultimately, the reason we were all in this situation was the fault of Adolf Hitler; we had all been innocent victims. The cost of wiping out Hitler and his Nazi sympathisers had cost so many innocent civilians and members of the armed forces of all nations, so much. Incredible how one man's lust for power and his own idealism can cause so much destruction.

Before taking us back to the airport, our transport took us to visit the Volkswagen V1 and V2 flying bomb factory near Hamburg. Next our driver took us to see what remained of the U-boat pens on the banks of the River Elbe. The structure of these buildings was unbelievable owing to the thickness of the concrete. The Nazis used POWs to work almost continually, pouring more and more concrete on to the roof of these structures so that they became almost impenetrable to aerial bombing. The bombs just literally bounced off the roof. Finally, in April 1945, 617 Squadron, using specially designed bombs called "Grand Slam" and "Tallboy" managed to impact the structure of the U-boat pens in Hamburg. On 2nd May, knowing that the Allies would soon capture the pens, the Germans blew them up themselves, using depth charges from within. On 11th November 1945 British Army Royal Engineers detonated several well-placed explosives in an attempt to implode the whole complex.

A few days later, we were back on another "Cooks Tour", this time with our normal pilot Squadron Leader Rogers, tasked with touring Cologne, Wuppertal and the Mohne Dam near Dortmund.

As we flew over the Mohne Dam, we could still see the repaired section of the dam wall that had been replaced after the destruction caused by the Dambusters. Mohne Dam had been the first dam to be breached by the bouncing bomb invented by the British engineer, Barnes Wallis. On the night of 16th May 1943, 617 Squadron based at RAF Scampton and led by 24-year old Wing Commander Guy Gibson, completed the famous Dambuster raid. The crews were multi-national with members from Canada, Australia, New Zealand, USA and Great Britain. During their raid they bombed the Mohne, Eder, Sorpe and Ennepe dams.

All these dams were used to provide electricity to the Ruhr Valley, which was the industrial heartland of Germany at the time. Guy's Lancaster led the 19 Lancaster attack on the dams. The first target was Mohne; Guy's aircraft did the first run, but the bomb landed short and did not impact the dam's wall. Instead of turning for home, Guy then used his aircraft as a decoy, by flying along the dam wall to draw gunfire away from the incoming bombers. The Mohne Dam was finally breached on the fifth attack. The remaining aircraft then moved on to Eder Dam, which was breached on the fourth attempt. The remaining targeted dams of Sorpe and Ennepe were attacked by the limited number of aircraft still carrying bombs, but there were insufficient bombs left to breach these. The destruction of the Mohne and Eder dams caused catastrophic flooding, horrendously killing over 1,300 civilians including a large number of POWs, who were made to work in the area's factories.

Those who survived had to cope with a scarcity of clean drinking water and the destruction of their homes and the factories in which they had worked. It must have been devastating for those poor people, but the destruction of two hydroelectric power stations and the local workforce that manned the industry had a huge impact upon the Nazi war machine. These dams had been bombed several times previously by normal bombs that had made no impact on the wall structure; the bouncing bomb was the only weaponry capable of destroying the dam walls.

The Dambuster raid became legendary amongst the Allies worldwide, mainly because it was a combination of strategic warfare, achieved through ground breaking science, coupled with incredible flying skill and bravery that attained a huge targeted impact against the enemy with just 19 bombers and their crews.

Guy Gibson was awarded the Victoria Cross for his bravery in deflecting fire from the incoming bombers. All the crews involved in this raid knew the odds were stacked against them as they had to fly in over the target against the fire of anti-aircraft guns at a height of only 60 ft. Only eighty of the 133 aircrew who conducted this raid survived. Thirty-two of these brave men were later killed in further operations throughout the war, but forty-eight of the original Dambuster crew members survived the war. Sadly, Guy Gibson did not survive, as tragically he was shot down on 19th September 1944, by friendly fire when a Lancaster gunner opened fire on the Mosquito Guy was flying, mistaking it for a Junkers 88.

Another tour that we made included an aerial inspection of the Channel Islands. Located just off the French coast of Normandy, the Channel Islands are not officially part of Great Britain, but Jersey and Guernsey are Crown Dependencies similar to the Isle of Man. The Germans had obviously been worried that the Allies might use these islands as a stepping-stone for invasion into northern France, so to prevent this they invaded the Channel Islands on 30th June 1940 and continued to occupy them until VE Day. My pilot, Squadron Leader Rogers, had some connection with the tiny Channel Island of Sark. I can remember him talking about it before we boarded the Lancaster on this particular tour. We took aerial photographs of all the Channel Islands, but flew particularly low over Sark so that he could point out certain features to us. Sark is the smallest of the four main Channel Islands, being just over two square miles in size with a population of about 500, yet the Germans placed 350 soldiers on Sark during the war. Sark, to this day, still has no runway, no tarmac roads and no motorised vehicles other than a few tractors. The only form of transport is horse and cart.

Seeing Sark reminded me of Heligoland, which we had been sent to bomb during the war. When we were told our target in the briefing, we all looked a bit shocked as Heligoland was pretty much the German equivalent of Sark. Sadly for the occupants of this tiny peaceful island, Hitler had selected Heligoland as a site to build huge U-boat pens and as such it was a major target for us. Thankfully, most of the inhabitants survived the war as the bombs were all targeted on the U-boat pens.

On 24th July 1945 our crew did our first sortie as part of Operation Dodge, which was collecting our troops (mainly from the 8th Army) and POWs from Italy. We were used to flying over northern Europe, but had never flown this distance before. We set off on our first ever flight to Italy at 6:30am, in aircraft LS "H", but we didn't get very far. Very early into our flight we developed a minor mechanical fault and were forced to divert into RAF Stradishall to get it fixed.

It took three hours for the ground crew to fix our Lancaster so we relaxed in the mess, but I remember we were quite fidgety to get going. We finally got airborne again at 10:40 and set course direct for Bari on the Adriatic coastline of Italy. The first part of our journey was common territory for us, flying over northern France, but soon we were plotting our course across Switzerland and into northern Italy. Our route took us over Mount Vesuvius and we decided to fly right over the top to have a good look. Vesuvius is just south east of Naples; its height changes with each eruption and has been recorded as anything from 3,891ft to 4,203ft above sea level. In March 1944, in the midst of the war, it had erupted and was still looking fairly menacing over a year later. We had all learned about Mount Vesuvius in our history lessons as children, and the destruction it had caused in AD79 when it erupted destroying Pompeii, so we were fascinated to have a close look at it. It was an incredible experience peering out of a Lancaster bomber, looking down into the crater of a recently erupted volcano and I even managed to take a photograph of it with my small box camera. We were all in wonder of it until suddenly we felt its might as the volcano pulled the aircraft down into its mouth. Our pilot had to apply full power and a nose up attitude to get us clear and there were a few moments when we all thought we wouldn't make it. We decided to give the volcano a bit more distance on our journey home.

Bari and Pomigliano were the two pick-up points for Operation Dodge, but our squadron was only collecting soldiers from Bari, an industrial port in southern Italy. Those trips were like a holiday to us, and we spent our free time there swimming in the Adriatic Sea, lazing about on the beach and eating good food. I always took my boxing gloves with me, usually managed to find someone to act as a sparring partner and would spend a lot of my leisure time working away at my skills and fitness.

On each occasion we returned with twenty soldiers as passengers. They all put up with the uncomfortable travelling conditions remarkably well. It can't have been very pleasant sitting on the floor with your back against the metal fuselage, cold, cramped and draughty, with four Merlin engines roaring the whole way home and with no ear defenders. A surprising number of them also experienced airsickness, but nonetheless they were all delighted to be flown home, rather than the alternative of being shipped home, which took considerably longer. It was very rewarding safely delivering soldiers back home. We would fly the soldiers into RAF Tibenham where a special army base with full facilities had been prepared for them.

We made several trips out to Bari as part of Operation Dodge. We flew out on 2nd September, returning on 6th, went out again on 11th, returning on 14th and then out again on 29th September returning on 1st October. We still mainly operated with our original pilot, Squadron Leader Rogers, but on occasions would fly with a different pilot. This included being flown by Wing Commander Nigel MacFarlane, DSO who at the time was the Commanding Officer of 15 Squadron at RAF Mildenhall. We also flew with other pilots from our squadron; Flt Officer Woodcock, Flt Lt Beech, Flt Lt Graham, Flt Lt Cook and Flt Officer Darlow. On one occasion we took a small detour to fly over the beautiful island of Sicily and Mount Etna on the east coast of this pretty island. Etna is the largest active volcano in Europe, but after our experience flying over Vesuvius, we were very respectful of volcanoes and gave Etna a wide berth, but it was a beautiful sight.

We all enjoyed these trips out to Bari collecting troops. Each time we would stay there for just a few days, sleeping at night under mosquito nets and enjoying the lovely warm climate - going for walks, swimming in the sea and sun bathing. We even managed to visit one of the beautiful vineyards in the area. I had read all about vineyards in school, but never thought I would get the opportunity to travel and see these things for myself. It was fascinating being in such a beautiful country and seeing both the similarities and the differences in their way of life. I remember that there was a railway line at the bottom of the runway and it was fascinating seeing how full the trains were. Those who could not squeeze into the carriages climbed up onto the carriage roofs, while others clambered onto the carriage step and clung on to the side of the carriage as it trundled along. The train would always sound its whistle as it passed the end of the runway. I wondered if this was to warn landing aircraft to keep out of its way, which made me smile.

We really enjoyed all the tasty fruits from Italy and would always bring some home with us. I can remember Pete and I were back at base in Mildenhall and had gone for a stroll through the town. We were walking along the footpath eating a pomegranate, which we had brought back from Italy with us a few days before. A lady stopped to ask where we had purchased it. Pete couldn't help himself and told her we had just bought it from the local grocer's shop. Rationing was still in force and fresh fruit was hard to come by. The lady looked at us aghast and said she had just left the shop and had specifically asked the shopkeeper for fresh fruit. She said he had told her that he only had apples. Pete said he must just keep them under the counter for his special customers. This sent the lady into an indignant tirade about how she was one of his most loyal and long-standing customers and she stormed off in the direction of the shop. We had visions of her demanding to search under his counter, poor man!

Repatriating soldiers from Bari in Italy.

A post-war view of the bombed bridges across the Rhine at Cologne.

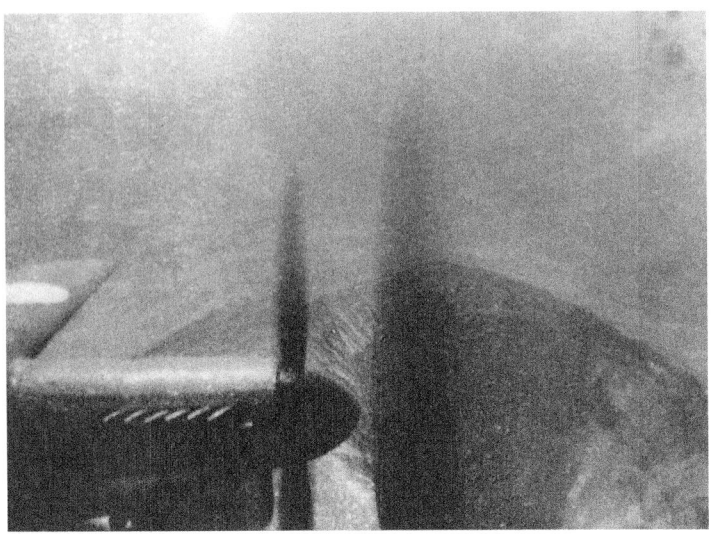

Flying over Mount Vesuvius!

An Avro Lincoln of 15 Squadron.

CHAPTER 23

TIGER FORCE

I n July 1945, US President Harry Truman, the British Prime Minister Winston Churchill and Soviet Russia's premier, Joseph Stalin held what became known as The Potsdam Conference. This meeting between the leaders of the three main Allied countries went on for a couple of weeks. The conference was held at the New Palace, situated on the River Havel, in Potsdam, south west of Berlin. The conference's main objectives were to sort out issues relating to post-war Europe and form policies regarding the war with Japan. On 26th July the three leaders issued a declaration demanding "unconditional surrender" from Japan. They were all aware that the Japanese culture expected every soldier to fight until the last man standing. Not much remained of the Japanese army, but it was obvious that this war could easily become a long drawn out conflict, which none of these leaders relished nor could afford.

Whilst Churchill was away in Potsdam, the general election took place in Britain and to everyone's amazement, Churchill did not get re-elected. So on 26th July 1945 (right at the end of this important conference), Clement Attlee found himself thrown into the Potsdam Conference as Britain's new Prime Minister.

Whilst these major world leaders met in conference, our preparation for operations out in the Pacific progressed. As part of our training we had to complete an escape exercise. The whole idea was to see how we would cope, lost in unfamiliar territory. We were driven through the night in the back of RAF transport vehicles and dropped off in the middle of a forest goodness knows where. The only thing we were given was a map of the local area with which to find our way to a tiny barn in the middle of the countryside, near Newmarket in Suffolk. We were not told where our current position was on the map. In addition to having to find out our whereabouts and then navigate to the tiny barn, we were also informed that we would be hunted by RAF military police pretending to be the enemy. We had no clue where we had been driven to and were completely disorientated.

Most of the aircrew went off in pairs, but a few, like myself, decided to go it alone. It was a really dark night, with no moonlight at all. I soon got out of the wooded area and was hoping that there would be a bit more natural light in the open fields, but there was none. I was literally just stumbling along in the dark, following one set compass heading hoping that at some point I would come across a landmark which I could identify on the map. As I made my way across a field of long, dew damp grass, I suddenly went flying as I tripped over a rope. As I lay flat of my face in the wet grass, I suddenly heard the terrifying noise of an angry bull which was attached to the rope and which I could sense was lying only a short distance from me. I have never moved so fast in my life and I didn't look back to see if I was being chased, all I hoped for was that the rope tether was both short and sturdy. I finally allowed myself the risk of slowing down and soon ascertained that the bull had been even more bewildered than me and so thankfully hadn't taken chase. As my heart rate slowed down a little, I settled back onto my compass heading.

Still following the direction of the compass, I passed through a farmyard and disturbed some geese. Their noise must have roused the farmer who emerged from a dimly lit rear door of the farmhouse firing a gun. No doubt the farmer must have thought the intruder was a fox or even a poacher.

Having safely escaped the farmyard, I found a ditch to hide in for a while whilst I worked out my location based upon the farm and the shape of the road I was on. Once I worked out where I was it dawned on me that I was currently only a few miles from West Row, where Barbara lived. I couldn't help myself - the temptation to see my girlfriend was too great, so I immediately got out of my ditch and navigated my way straight to her house. It was still the early hours of the morning when I arrived and I did not want to disturb any of the occupants, so I just let myself in through the back door, which I knew was always left unlocked. Tired and weary, I fell asleep on the sofa, but was soon roused by members of the family. They prepared me a bath, whilst Barbara's mother Rose, tidied up my clothing and found me some pyjamas, made me some breakfast and then ushered me upstairs to a comfortable bed, where I slept all day until almost nightfall. Once I was up and dressed, we all sat down for a lovely evening meal whilst I waited for the cover of dark to set off again.

During our meal, Barbara's father Gordon, asked me about the destination I had been tasked to find. I showed him the map and explained that although I knew how to find my way to Newmarket, I had no idea how to find this particular tiny barn in the middle of a field on the outskirts of the town. I also explained that being so close to RAF Mildenhall, there was every chance I would be picked up by the military police, acting as the enemy. He had a quick glance at the map and immediately announced that he not only knew the barn and the farmer who owned it, but he also knew exactly how to get there undetected.

As I finished my meal Gordon worked out the best route across the fields. I absolutely loved and admired Gordon Ford; what a pleasure it was to spend time with this gentleman, who just seemed to be at one with the countryside and everything in it. He just had this wonderful calm and caring nature that made all animals and humans instantly trust him.

I wanted to arrive at the barn under the cover of darkness before sunrise. Gordon reckoned it would take us about four hours to get there, so we decided to set off at midnight. In the meantime, I sat relaxing in the comfort of their lovely home, chatting to my beautiful girlfriend. I couldn't help but smile to myself thinking of my colleagues who had probably spent a very uncomfortable day camouflaged in a ditch somewhere, most likely without any food and just a bit of river water to drink.

The route Gordon chose took us down a narrow path along a section of the River Lark, across many arable fields that looked close to harvesting and meadows full of sleepy cattle. He knew all the farmers who worked the land; some were relatives, others close friends. He knew all the livestock in the fields, their breeding programmes and the history behind each herd. He knew all the crops growing, when they would be due for harvest and what would be growing in that field next year. He would point out a fox burrow and a badger's den as we passed by and his favourite hunting areas for catching rabbits and fish. Being with Gordon always pulled me back to my wonderful childhood memories of my walks to school with my brother and sister through similar countryside. It had been a wonderful education in its own right and so was spending time with Gordon.

We walked the last section in companionable silence, with me close behind, quite literally walking in my future father-in-law's footsteps. As we came out of a small wooded area, I was still walking with my head down, but my peripheral vision could tell that dawn was fast approaching. It was still extremely dark, but there was just that hint that things would soon be about to awaken and then from somewhere nearby I heard a cockerel crowing. Right at that moment Gordon stopped, opened the field gate and pointed to a line of poplar trees in the field opposite and said: "Your destination is just beyond those trees. The best of luck." I could not thank this man enough for the way he had put himself out for me, but I had a feeling that he had enjoyed the challenge even more than I had. Gordon was a legend of a man and I can sincerely say that I never ever heard anyone have a bad word to say about him, nor him of others. It was a privilege to have known him and to have spent moments like this together.

Before he left me, Gordon told me that the best way into the barn undetected would be through a back door which he reliably informed me was always left unlocked. I waved him goodbye and worked my way around to the barn and the back door. I lifted the latch and true to Gordon's word the door creaked open. I strolled in and found an RAF officer and an RAF sergeant on duty. The look of surprise on their faces almost made me laugh. They weren't expecting anyone to arrive so soon and I must have looked immaculate having spent the whole day sleeping, well fed and very clean and fresh. After their initial gasped surprise, they both soon rallied and congratulated me on being the first one to have made it. After they had taken all my particulars and given me a cup of tea, I was transported back to RAF Mildenhall where I had a good meal and went to bed.

I don't think many others made it to the barn, they were mainly all captured by the pretend enemy. Not many chose to talk about their experiences during this training task and I heard that a large number of the aircrew registered complaints to RAF headquarters concerning how they were treated when they were "captured". Apparently, they were subjected to intense interrogation by the RAF Special Police, which had been based upon reports of how the Japanese conducted interrogation. Apparently, the Japanese used techniques that did not comply with the rules laid down by the Geneva Convention. The more reports I heard about the horrors of that training event the more I decided it was best to keep my little trip to my girlfriend's house a secret.

In preparation for Operation Tiger Force we were given lectures by a special agent who had experience of Japanese warfare. The main topic covered was the difference to expect from Japanese warfare as opposed to Nazi warfare. We were told that whilst the Nazis had on many occasions ignored the Geneva Convention, 95% of POWs did make it home alive after the war. The Japanese on the other hand had refused to even acknowledge the Geneva Convention's legislation concerning the treatment of POWs. Captured soldiers, ground crew and civilians were used as slave labour in mines and to build the railway link between Thailand and Burma. Many were dying due to the backbreaking work, unsanitary conditions and starvation. We were told that as aircrew we would be treated more as spies rather than as normal POWs and as such we should avoid capture at all costs. They explained that all aircrew going into combat would be issued with a cyanide capsule and were advised that the best place to keep it was in the anus. If we crash-landed, we were told to fight to the death and not to surrender. If capture was inevitable, then we were strongly advised to commit suicide by taking the cyanide capsule, as once swallowed, it promised instant death which we were told was definitely more desirable than death by Japanese torture.

We were briefed on all the information currently held about the Japanese kamikaze (suicide pilots), which was a form of warfare unheard of before. All of these pilots were well educated, the elite of Japanese youth, and were normally recruited whilst still at university. A whole class of students would be called in for a briefing and told that they had been selected and could now volunteer to become kamikaze pilots. At the end of the briefing they were told what a privilege it was and the statement was made: "Surely there is no one here who does not wish to volunteer?" To refuse at this point would bring ruination to both the student and his family. Once all their training was complete and they were called upon to make their final flight, there was still really no choice. The alternative was to disobey orders, be branded a coward, and be given the choice to either commit hara-kiri, a ritual of suicide by disembowelling, or to be shot by their commanding officers. They would die knowing that their family would also suffer humiliation.

Before their final flight the commanding officer would give each pilot a small drink, and toast them with the words: "You are now a god, free from all earthly desires. I wish you success." The pilots would drink a toast to each other, and make a final toast to the Emperor Hirohito, at the same time bowing towards the Imperial Palace. Each pilot would then wrap a white scarf called a hachimaki, which had a hand-stitched sun, around his forehead.

The officer taking our class explained that the Japanese emperor was looked upon as a god and that he expected everyone in Japan to fight to the death to protect him. Even civilians would commit suicide rather than have the dishonour of being captured. All civilians had armed themselves, even if it was just with sharpened bamboo sticks, to use in combat against the Allied forces. The officer explained that the war with Japan was destined to be a long and bloody one as every man, woman and child was determined to fight to the death with no surrender.

CHAPTER 24

ATOMIC WARFARE

Our Tiger Force training was now complete and we were informed that the long-awaited Lincoln bomber had received operational status and should be arriving shortly; but then we received the news that completely rocked the world.

On 6th August 1945 at 8:15am US President Harry S Truman gave the go ahead to drop an atomic bomb on the city of Hiroshima, with a population of over 300,000 people. This was the first time that an atomic bomb had ever been used in warfare. The devastation was immense. It is estimated that over 135,000 people lost their lives that morning. The world looked on in horror.

Despite the enormity of this bombing, Japan still refused to surrender, maintaining that it would fight on until the last man standing. Truman then ordered a second city to be bombed. The Boeing B-29 Superfortress bomber, which the crew had named Bockscar, took off at 3:40am on 9th August 1945 with the aim of dropping an atomic bomb, named "Fat Man" on the city of Kokura. On route the aircraft developed a fuel problem that meant they were very tight on fuel, so it was decided to go for the secondary target of Nagasaki instead. Strange how the fate of thousands of citizens of both cities was determined by a fuel feed problem. Tragically, a further 87,000 people died that day in Nagasaki. The power blast of these two atomic bombs was the equivalent of all the bombs that had been dropped on Great Britain during the Blitz.

The USA then gave the Japanese the option to surrender or have more atomic bombs dropped on other major cities. The warning had the desired effect as on 14th August 1945 Japan finally surrendered, and so ended World War 2.

The relief that the war was finally over was overwhelming, but we also felt horror too. Two whole cities in Japan had been annihilated. You couldn't help but grieve for humanity. We had witnessed the carnage of war, lived through the devastation of our towns and cities during the Blitz and then walked the streets of Hamburg and Berlin and seen the damage that our own bombs had caused in Germany. Witnessing that was cruel enough, but the knowledge that there now existed a single bomb capable of wiping out a whole city was frightening. It felt unnerving to contemplate that the devastation caused by our bombs had occurred over five years and taken thousands of aircraft and their crews, yet a far bigger blow had been dealt to Japan by two US bomber aircraft using only two bombs. Although this atomic weapon had been used in our defence, it was still totally unnerving. We had already seen the horror that one crazed individual with a lust for power could evoke on the world with normal ammunition, but now that this form of warfare existed, God save us from future despots.

Barbara and I, Pete and Pearl, and Pearl's sister Joy were all on holiday in Arundel when we heard the news that the war with Japan was over. Prior to this announcement we had been expecting to be sent out to Okinawa fairly imminently, so we had taken the opportunity to have a few precious days away.

Pearl had a relative who owned a small guesthouse in Arundel, so we opted to book a short holiday there. We booked to go by train and it was so exciting getting on the train together. The girls looked stunning in their summer dresses and I just couldn't believe how beautiful Barbara was, but it wasn't just that, she also had such a lovely gentle demeanour and great poise. I was extremely proud that she was my girlfriend. I hadn't had a girlfriend before and I was Barbara's first boyfriend too. I can remember how happy the five of us were, and the excited conversation and endless laughter as the train rattled its way southbound towards Arundel. Even the weather was beautiful. Nothing could have broken the mood of excitement and happiness we all felt.

Every moment together felt special as Pete and I were not sure when we would see the girls again for quite some time.

Once we got off the train it was about a ten-minute walk to the guesthouse. The guesthouse was small, but extremely comfortable and we received a very warm welcome. The girls settled into their room and Pete and I were shown ours. Once we had unpacked, we met downstairs for our evening meal and then sat up late into the night chatting and joking. The next morning, after a hearty breakfast, we decided to go for a stroll through the town and take a look at the castle. We were just about to set off, when the guesthouse owners told us we had best come and listen to the news on the radio.

We were absolutely dazed by the news. We had no real concept of just how much devastation had been caused by the atomic bombs; all we could focus on at the time was that Japan had surrendered. World War 2 was finally over. As we strolled through Arundel the newspaper billboards were all full of the news: "Japan - unconditional surrender", "Victory in Japan VJ Day".

The relief that we wouldn't be facing combat against the Japanese was incredible, but now that it was officially over you finally had time to reflect upon the deep sorrow that was locked inside you too. Whilst you are in active combat you have to stay focused on keeping yourself going, you cannot allow deep emotions to overwhelm you and stop you from completing your task. Once that task is achieved and the burden is lifted, you can finally allow yourself time for reflection and emotion.

As thankful as I was to have survived, I also had the deepest of sorrow for all those who had not. I was suddenly swamped by the immense sadness that I had previously buried deep inside me, for all the aircrew I had befriended, laughed and joked with, never to be forgotten, who I would never see again. They would never see this day, yet without them, this day would never have been. Bomber Command lost 55,573 young men who would never get the chance to walk arm in arm with their girlfriends, in the sunshine.

I could still recall countless friends, their jokes and banter; remember their mannerisms, their fears and their hopes for the future that was stolen from them. I wished I could just say to them: "Your sacrifice wasn't wasted, we did it, we not only kept Britain's freedom, but we also helped to restore peace for much of the world too". Such great, talented young men.It was a privilege to have known them, and I felt a responsibility to them that they should not be forgotten. John 15:13 in the Bible states: "Greater love hath no man than this, that a man lay down his life for his friends." For this I thanked every one of them. It felt wrong to feel so happy enjoying my freedom when it had cost so many lives to secure.

This poem has always stayed with me:

Amidst rejoicing let us pause, for some were left on foreign shores
And some the mighty ocean kept. Remember them and those who wept."

We went back to the guesthouse for our lunch and then settled down in the guests' living room to listen to the Prime Minister, Clement Attlee's official VJ Day speech on the radio, in which he declared a three-day national holiday of celebration:

> *"For the moment let all who can relax and enjoy themselves in the knowledge of work well done. Peace has once again come to the world. Let us thank God for this great deliverance and His Mercy. Long live* the King.*"*

The radio report also informed us that the US President Truman had said:

> *"This is the day we have been waiting for since Pearl Harbour."*

The following day we decided to go for a walk around the local area. The route we planned looked like it had a railway crossing, but when we arrived there was no designated crossing area, but neither was there any fence to prevent you walking across it. Pete and I didn't really give it a moment's thought, we just listened and looked out for trains and then made our way across the track carefully jumping over the electrified lines. I glanced back watching Barbara, Pearl and Joy doing the same following close behind. We all stopped to watch and listen before setting off over the second set of electrified lines. While we were paused in the middle of the lines, I just happened to say how dangerous it was that the lines were unprotected by a fence or even a bank, as it would be so easy for anyone, but especially children and animals, to be killed by the electrified lines. The girls all looked aghast as they had not realised that the lines were electrified. It had only been good fortune that all three of them had just mimicked what Pete and I had done. The girls were far more careful as they jumped over the remaining lines. It was frightening to think how close I had come to losing Barbara just by being careless. We finished our walk and returned to the guesthouse by a different route.

After my wonderful few days away in Arundel with Barbara and our friends, surrounded by the excitement of VJ Day, it was now time to return back to base. The mood on the base was peculiar; we were all congratulating one another that the war was finally over, but we all felt a bit bewildered really, almost an anti-climax. I had spent the whole of my adult life living for nothing else but to serve my country in combat, living off adrenaline and banter and now suddenly it was all over and I felt at a loose end.

My twenty-first birthday in September 1945 was a time of decision-making. I remember having many sleepless nights trying to decide what was best for me to do. I had been with the same crew since we all first met at RAF Little Horwood in July 1944. We'd only been together as a crew for 14 months, but what an intense time we had endured together. Only those who are thrown together in such challenging situations can ever truly appreciate how it feels when your team disbands. They had all decided to take the option to demobilise and return to their old professions. My parents had expressed their wish that I should do the same and return home and wrote to inform me that my brother was already demobbed and back home.

Things weren't quite so simple for me and I was torn. I wanted to go home, but I absolutely did not want to leave my girlfriend Barbara. I knew Barbara was the one for me, but she was still only 17 and her family wanted her to wait a while before making such a huge commitment. I was also still enjoying flying, but I knew I would probably never form the same bond with a new crew.

We were all called for an individual interview with an RAF officer to discuss our future. I can still remember sitting outside his office dithering as to what I should do. The officer talked through my options as my head whirled. He ran through the options if I decided to remain in the RAF as well as openings currently available to bomber aircrew wishing to demob. The main occupations that interested me were training as a civil airline pilot or a merchant seaman wireless operator. Or I could take a short course and become a schoolteacher as they were still in very short supply. I fancied the civil airline job the most, but knew that this would most likely take me away from Barbara again. There was also the risk that signing up to remain in the RAF could mean that I might be stationed elsewhere too.

After giving careful consideration of the advice provided, I decided to sign on and remain in the RAF for a few more years, and just hope that I could remain stationed at RAF Mildenhall.

Now that Operation Tiger Force was officially cancelled, there was no longer a rush to move the squadron on to the Lincoln bombers, but we were informed that the changeover would still be going ahead over the next year, (15 Squadron finally took delivery of Lincoln bombers in February 1947). As part of this changeover, any aircraft that had seen heavy duty during the war were destined to be scrapped.

I can remember how sad and indignant we all felt when, on 13th December 1945, we were instructed to make a ferry flight, taking Lancaster LS J for "Jig" to its graveyard in Waddington. This aircraft was 15 Squadron's lucky aircraft, having successfully completed a total of 134 bombing operations. We had all been delighted that "Jig" had survived the war and yet now, even though it was still fully serviceable, it was being sent to Waddington to be scrapped. Anything that had survived the war, we felt, should be allowed to live on. It was hard for us to shut that aircraft down after its last ever flight and walk away. We were all very quiet and subdued as we did it. To us it felt like shooting an old faithful warhorse.

Avro Lincoln RF423 LS-E, of 15 Squadron.

CHAPTER 25

DIGGING DEEP

To mark the official end of World War 2 the government arranged a special celebration in London, called the London Victory Celebrations, on 8th June 1946. As I had served during the war I was invited to attend and was allowed to take a guest. I obviously chose to take Barbara. As I had been a wartime aircrew member, we were allotted preferential seating. It was a privilege to see so many nationalities that had been our allies and we had the opportunity to talk to a number of them and learn about their experiences. It turned out to be a most memorable day with the weather being exceptionally bright and the sun continually shining. There was a long parade of service personnel and fabulous military bands, including the massed pipers of the Scottish and Irish regiments. On the dais taking the salute were King George VI and his wife Queen Elizabeth, their two daughters Princess Elizabeth and Princess Margaret and the King's mother Queen Mary. Clement Attlee and Winston Churchill were also on the podium.

In the evening, London looked spectacular - illuminated by floodlights, large crowds gathered along the banks of the River Thames and on Westminster Bridge to watch King George VI and other members of the Royal party going down the river on the royal barge. The evening ended with a beautiful firework display. It had been such a long time since we had all seen fireworks and it was just lovely to see the London sky lit up with the colour and beauty of fireworks rather than bombs and fire. It was a fantastic atmosphere and we were so grateful to have been invited to be part of it.

In July 1946 I was informed that I would soon be moving base to RAF Wyton near St Ives in Cambridgeshire. It was only 30 miles from West Row and Barbara, but it still felt like a big wrench having to move away. 15 Squadron had been based at RAF Wyton a couple of times before in its history, but the reason for our move was to make way for the USSAF, who had been allocated Mildenhall as a new US base. RAF Mildenhall was given a complete overhaul and wasn't fully operational again until July 1950. At least at RAF Wyton we were no longer billeted in Nissen huts, but instead had proper sleeping quarters in purpose-built accommodation, but still no bedside lamps!

It was fortunate that our accommodation was up-graded, as the winter of 1946 to 1947 was to be the harshest we had ever experienced with Thursday 23rd January being the coldest day in Britain for fifty years. This was followed by six weeks of extremely heavy snowfall, with easterly winds driving the loose snow into massive snowdrifts, many up to twenty-foot high. The temperature dropped as low as 16 degrees Fahrenheit (-9 degrees Celsius).

Non-stop blizzards stopped shipping in the English Channel and fishing fleets were confined to ports. On 20th February, the cross-channel ferry service from Dover to Ostend was cancelled due to a huge ice pack along the Belgian coastline. Ice floes were also reported off the coast of East Anglia. All the major rivers in Britain froze including the River Thames in London.

The whole country virtually shut down as very few roads or railway lines were open. Some snow drifts rendered roads and rail tracks completely impassable for long stretches, up to 20 miles in some cases. The armed forces were called upon to try to keep some vital roads and rail links open and to try to rescue those who were stranded, but with no mobile phones to call for emergency help it was a risky business setting off on a journey so radio stations repeatedly warned people to stay indoors. Many women had to cope with giving birth at home with just their family or neighbours for assistance.

After all the resilience shown during the war, civilians across the country had to dig deep one last time to endure one of the worst winters on record.

Food, coal and commodities were in short supply for many years after the war and because of this rationing was still in place. Therefore, few households had much produce stocked in their cupboards or coal in their scuttles. Those who managed to venture out to restock soon found that coal was very difficult to come by.

Clement Attlee's Labour government was in power at the time and it was heavily criticised by the public as it had recently nationalised the coal industry. Historically, coal suppliers always kept large stockpiles of coal in case of a sudden increase in demand or a period of interruption in coal mining. Under the new government control these stockpiles had been allowed to greatly diminish. At the time when the snow blizzards hit Britain, there was only sufficient coal stockpiled to run the country for approximately four weeks. The snowstorms raged on for six weeks. Transporting the coal was also a logistical nightmare and despite the Armed Forces best efforts, trainloads of precious coal became stranded on railway tracks blocked by snowdrifts. Even trying to access the coal became extremely challenging as the stockpiles had just become hard frozen snow-covered mountains. The situation was exacerbated as the extreme low temperatures meant demand had escalated.

Electricity was also threatened due to the acute shortage of coal to power the electricity stations, so the government imposed lots of restrictions on the use of electricity.

Radio transmissions were reduced to only a few broadcasts each day; newspapers were severely cut down in size as well as in the amount produced. Most magazines were ordered to stop printing, to reduce the energy used in producing them and the use of electricity for lighting was also greatly restricted. People were encouraged to go back to using candles for lighting, to minimise electrical usage. A heavy fine of £100 or even up to three months imprisonment was threatened for anyone not abiding by these restrictions.

With a very limited supply of both coal and electricity, much of the country was left literally freezing to death, in the semi-darkness of candlelight, without even the entertainment of the radio. Many were without water too due to frozen or burst pipes.

I was lucky living on an RAF base that had large stores of food and fuel, but I didn't particularly worry about Barbara and her family or my family either. I had no means of communicating with either household as neither had a telephone. I expected my family would be fine as they lived in a fairly built-up area with plenty of help at hand and my mother was a very resourceful lady. Barbara's family were in a more rural spot, but they did have good neighbours, plus, Gordon, Barbara's father, was extremely good at providing for his family in difficult circumstances. Gordon kept his family and friends extremely well fed throughout the war, by catching roach, pike and carp from the local streams. I doubted he'd be able to hunt during these conditions, but knew that no matter what the weather, Gordon would find a way to keep his family warm, fed and safe.

The initial relief of the thaw was soon superseded by the devastation of the floods, particularly during the month of March. Vast numbers of rivers burst their banks including the

River Thames, which left large areas of Windsor and Eton under water and looking more like Venice than London. Residents in flooded areas had to retreat upstairs and wait for food supplies to be delivered by the rescue services in small boats. All the Armed Services were required to help get emergency provisions to people stranded and homeless. Those living on higher ground escaped the flooding, but many now found themselves stranded on their small island of high ground so also needed help with provisions. As the majority of households didn't have telephones, those in remote areas had to rely on rescue services just perceiving that they might have a problem.

Our squadron was deployed to drop food packages to the more remote areas and villages that had otherwise become inaccessible. It was strange flying over the British countryside with its geography so altered by the flooding; so much of it was under water with lots of small islands of high ground. We flew low level in order to be able to assess areas that looked like they required assistance. People would often come rushing out waving frantically at us so we would report their location to the rescue services. On high ground you would see small groups of farm animals and horses that had managed to survive.

Back at base we had people seeking refuge, camping in every spare room. RAF Wyton, like many other military bases, was used to provide temporary shelter for families who had been evacuated from their homes.

As the snow melted it slowly unveiled the sorrowful death and destruction that it had caused. It was estimated that over

70,000 acres of wheat and 80,000 tons of potatoes, along with many other crops, were all destroyed. This was extremely bad news for a nation still surviving on rations. Much more horrifying though, was the tragic loss of farm animals. A quarter of all the sheep in Britain died due to the severe conditions either through the freeze or afterwards due to the floods. As the snow melted it revealed whole flocks of sheep that had sadly frozen to death. In Wales many farmers lost their entire flock, so the government had to issue a disaster fund to help keep farmers and their families ticking over whilst they gained new stock and started new breeding programmes. Despite this it apparently took Wales six years to replenish the sheep that died that winter.

The loss of so much livestock resulted in a huge shortage of meat, eggs, milk and all dairy products. Those who faired best were families with gardens they had converted to keep their own pigs, chickens, goats or even a cow. Most were able to provide sufficient shelter and food for just a few animals, some even converted a downstairs room in their homes to save their valuable livestock.

Industry also suffered as few people could get into the factories to work for a couple of months, first due to the snow and then the flooding. Those employees who lived locally and did manage to struggle into work, were often unable to be productive, due to a lack of fuel or materials, so were generally sent home, often without wages. Poor factory production resulted in a huge shortage of household commodities and after the thaw the black market thrived as people became desperate for supplies.

It was well over two months before I managed to get to see Barbara again. I finally got a few days leave and set off immediately to her house, just hoping that she would be there. When I arrived, she was at home and the whole family excitedly welcomed me in. It was so lovely to see Barbara again; just one look at those beautiful eyes made my heart melt.

As I had expected Gordon had kept his family, plus the pig at the bottom of their garden and their chickens, all well fed and warm throughout it all. We spent many happy hours discussing the extreme conditions and experiences. Barbara's mother, Rose, made us all tea and generally fussed over us and then cooked us a lovely evening meal. I will always remember that whenever Rose welcomed you in for tea, she would always ask: "Have you had your second cup?" Tea was rationed so that you were only allowed two cups, but she always wanted to make sure you didn't miss out. Even long after the rationing of tea had ended Rose would still always ask you if you'd had your second cup. What a wonderful warm-hearted lady she was.

Rose Ford, myself and Barbara outside our home in West Row, Suffolk.

CHAPTER 26

Rules of Engagement

When Barbara turned twenty, I decided it was time to get engaged. We had been dating now for three years, the war was over and life was far more settled. Barbara and I had discussed our intentions to one another and also hinted on many occasions in front of her family, but I now wanted to make it official. Barbara had met my family when she came with me once on one of my short visits back home to Padgate. I felt a trip back home to see my family was now long overdue and this seemed the ideal time to officially ask Barbara to marry me.

There was also a very practical reason why I wanted to share this moment with my family, and that was the extremely important matter of purchasing an engagement ring. Jewellery was very scarce at the time, and I knew that if anyone would have the contacts necessary to source a ring it would be my mother.

It was a long journey by train to get back home to Padgate, but journeys always flew by when Barbara was with me. As soon as we arrived and settled into our rooms, I quickly took my mother to one side, whispered my intention to her and asked if she knew where I would be able to buy an engagement ring. As I suspected, this was no problem at all for my mother. Jewellery was one of her passions and this was a task she relished. She asked me about sizing, so my next mission was to sneak into the spare bedroom, where Barbara was staying and get the small dress ring she wore on evenings out, from the dressing table. With this acquired, I made the excuse to Barbara that my mother needed some help to carry the groceries and then my mother and I set off on one of the most important trips of my life, to find my future wife a ring to cherish for a lifetime.

The jeweller's shop was one of the very few remaining in business after the war and the selection was very limited, but the owner of the shop did have a ring the correct size. It was perfect, a simple band of gold with three diamonds, known as a trinity or trilogy ring, as the three diamonds mean: "I loved you before, I love you now and I will love you forever".

I couldn't wait - as soon as my mother and I got back to the house, I rushed and found Barbara and immediately asked her to marry me. We both knew this day was intended, but it was still an exciting and wonderful moment to hear her say "Yes" and place the ring on her finger. It was a perfect fit and so lovely to be at home with my parents and my new fiancée. My mother excitedly sat down to write to my sister Cis in the USA and to my brother Herbert who was away working, to let them know the news.

Whilst I was home, I decided to take a trip over to my old school to see Mr Rice. I had always been grateful for everything he had helped me to achieve and I just wanted him to know how much I appreciated it. Whilst I was there, he asked me if I would be happy to talk to the children. He called them all into the main hall and I spent a couple of happy hours talking about some of my wartime experiences and my childhood in their school. The children asked lots of questions and it was lovely to have a quick tour of the school and see all my old haunts again.

Barbara and I spent a week with my family, and then it was time to travel home and share our exciting news with Barbara's family. Barbara couldn't wait to show off her new ring to all her friends and family.

I had such a wonderful extended leave, but now it was time to return to base. Most crew members were still on leave when I returned so the next few days were very quiet. I can recall sitting on my bed in an empty room thinking - what happens now? I had just got engaged and wanted to get married as soon as possible, but I was still in the RAF and not sure where I might be deployed next. I realised that since joining the RAF my job had been to follow orders, but now I needed to start taking control of my life and deciding my own future. For the first time in my life I didn't have a designated path ahead of me with a set focus, suddenly I had choices and it wasn't a nice feeling.

Fortunately, I had my boxing training to keep me occupied so I soon prised myself out of my malaise, pulled on my PT kit and set off for the gym. There are few things better than a boxer's punch ball to settle the mood. I needed to increase my training as I had been asked to represent the RAF Bomber Command as a middleweight boxer, competing for my squadron in the RAF Bomber Command Middleweight Championships.

On 24th April 1947 I was flown down to the RAF station at Llandow in South Wales to compete. The fights were scheduled to take place in the hangars at RAF St Athan, just a few minutes drive from Llandow airfield. It is amazing to me that, years later, I now live on a farm belonging to my daughter Caroline and her husband Jamie overlooking St Athan airfield. If you could have told me that in seventy-three years time I would be living on a farm nearby, I would have been astounded. Jimmy Wilde was our referee. It was a privilege to meet him, as he was considered to be one of the best flyweight boxers ever. He finished his days living in Barry, in the Vale of Glamorgan in South Wales, very close to my current home. I was the Bomber Command Middleweight Champion in 1946 and in 1947.

On my return from Wales, I had a few days off to recover from my boxing matches and then it was back into cross-country flight training in the Lincolns. Despite the fact that World War 2 had officially ended, there were still major problems and tensions in the world. One of the biggest tensions centred around Berlin. The Soviet Russians had captured Berlin at the end of the war, but during a post-war conference between the USA, Britain, France and Soviet Russia it was decided that it would be best to split Germany into four zones, with a section given to the USA, one section to Britain, another to France and one section to Soviet Russia. It was further decided that as Berlin was tactically an extremely important city, it should also be split into the same four sections, even though Berlin, was right in the middle of the Russian zone. The Russians were clearly uneasy about having such a prominent Western influence right in the middle of their quarter of Germany and quickly set up barbed wire fencing around their quarter of Berlin. The Berlin Wall wasn't built until much later, but the foundations of the unrest started then.

Soviet Russia and the USA had both shown their military supremacy during World War 2 and although they had fought as allies, their ideologies were vastly different.

Out of all the Allies, Soviet Russia suffered the greatest losses of both troops and civilians throughout the duration of the war and like all countries involved, suffered huge financial losses as well. Russia was determined to strip their part of Berlin and Germany of all its resources to help prop up their own economy, whereas the other Allies wanted their sections of Berlin to prosper in order that peace would reign and its people prosper under democracy.

Further friction grew as both Soviet Russia and the USA

were trying to encourage senior German weaponry scientists to relocate to their countries. These were the scientists who had worked on the German VI bombs and VII rockets. Guided missiles were seen to be the future of warfare weaponry. No one wanted mass indiscriminate bombing of whole cities, they wanted to be able to pinpoint specific strategic areas and launch their missiles at them from as far away from the target as possible. All the Allies were keen to view the German rocket factories, which were found to be a warfare technological treasure trove. This rush to amass more knowledge of weaponry caused more and more distrust between the USA and Soviet Russia.

All these factors combined to form what became known as the Cold War. Soviet Russia, the USA, Britain and the other countries never directly declared war against one another, but instead used other smaller conflicts around the world as a stage to show their own power and to weaken other countries' defences and resources. These conflicts always erupted wherever there were strategically important resources.

One of the countries where there was plenty of conflict was Egypt and our squadron were soon to be sent out to the RAF station in Shallufa, Egypt. The extra range of the Lincoln bombers made them ideal for this work and the Lancasters were now being totally phased out in favour of the Lincolns. I flew my last ever flight in a Lancaster bomber on 19th March 1947. It was registration number, LS D, flown by Flt Lt Williams, but I didn't have much time to dwell on it, as three days later we were back flying as a crew together again, but this time in a Lincoln bomber.

Our first flight out to Egypt on 2nd December 1947, felt like an epic journey and a grand adventure for seven young men in a Lincoln bomber. We didn't fly out as a squadron, but each aircraft went out individually as required.

On the way, we were scheduled to stop off overnight at RAF Castel Benito in Libya, before continuing our flight the following day across to Egypt. Libya was another troubled country because everyone wanted control of its oil. It had been occupied by Italy since 1911 before being captured by the British during World War 2 in 1943. RAF Castel Benito was situated near Libya's capital Tripoli. Understandably the Libyan people wanted control of their nation and their oil and this caused considerable tension. Service personnel were warned not to leave the confines of the airfield unless accompanied by an armed escort.

The next morning, we took off for RAF Shallufa. Our route took us across the northern part of the Sahara Desert, the largest desert in the world covering over three million square miles. RAF Shallufa was situated in the Sinai Peninsula.

Egypt had been a British Protectorate since 1914, until finally obtaining full independence from Great Britain in 1936. The only exception to this was the Suez Canal Zone which was still heavily guarded by British troops. The retention of our troops in the Suez Canal Zone had caused a lot of conflict that became known as the Suez Crisis or the Sinai War. The building of the Suez Canal had a huge impact on world trade as it connected the Mediterranean Sea to the Red Sea, which then led out into the Indian Ocean. Without the canal, ships would have to sail all the way down around the Cape of Good Hope, the southernmost point of Africa. Whoever controlled the Suez Canal had a hold over world trade. Britain was happy to relinquish control of Eygpt but wanted to keep control of this vital shipping route. Egypt understandably wanted to nationalise this valuable asset and take control of it.

It was my understanding that our Prime Minister Clement Attlee wanted to withdraw all our troops from Egypt, but Winston Churchill and a majority of MPs had been adamant that our troops should remain to protect our interests in the Suez Canal Zone, and prevent other countries overpowering the Egyptian military forces and taking over this region. The same argument was used concerning the Libyan oil fields. It was thought that the Libyan forces could easily be defeated and another country would soon take control, so this was why we were deployed to these countries - to maintain control over rebellious uprisings and show our presence to warn off other countries trying to seize these valuable assets. We didn't have a definite function, just merely to be there, show our force and to be ready at all times to take immediate action if ever it was deemed necessary.

RAF Shallufa was set right in the middle of a desert, so we didn't venture out much. Fortunately, the base was very well equipped with entertainment such as the Astra cinema and lots of sporting facilities. I kept myself busy with my boxing training. Experiencing my first sand storm was very surprising, we literally couldn't leave the building and sand got in everywhere. We were sent on sorties over the Sinai Desert to the east of Shallufa. I did enjoy flying over the desert; it was an extraordinary experience. Occasionally, we flew over a nomadic tribe with their camels travelling along unmarked routes with absolutely no discernible ground features on the landscape to navigate by. Despite our aerial view advantage, we relied totally on our technology and plotting skills so you couldn't help but marvel at these tribes, navigating across vast expanses of desert to their destination, finding watering holes along their way.

It was really interesting to meet local people who worked on the base. It always made me smile when we had our breaks as we would often sit outside sun bathing and they would be huddled in the boiler room because it was nice and warm in there.

As newcomers we were warned not to swim in the Sweet Water Canal near our base, as the water was highly contaminated. It was recommended that if anyone fell in the water that they should report sick immediately and be hospitalised. There was a small green island called Tewfiq Island, in the middle of the Sweet Water Canal. Tewfiq Island, stood out as a fabulous oasis with all its lush greenery, so as a result, it was a popular attraction to visit, but in order to do so, it was necessary to cross the inaccurately named, Sweet Water Canal. The only water transport were home-made rafts, made by some local

Our transport across the Sweet Water Canal, Egypt.

*In tropical uniform in Egypt.
(Original: hand-tinted B&W photograph).*

*In tropical uniform in Egypt.
(Original: hand-tinted B&W photograph).*

entrepreneurs from empty oil barrels and bits of wood. I could see why so many people fell into the canal, but having looked at and smelled the water I had no intention of being one of them. Each journey was precarious, being steered by one man with what appeared to be a long home-made paddle to move the contraption along. Each raft owner only charged a very small amount for this journey, but they were kept very busy.

Even though it was slightly off our flight path we were determined to take a small detour and fly over the pyramids and sphinx just outside Cairo. It was unbelievable to look out of our Lincoln bomber and see these incredible ancient monuments. I had learned all about them in school and seen pictures of them, but to actually fly over them was surreal.

A short while after we had arrived at RAF Shallufa, we were informed of a good, reliable and reasonably priced tailor, who spoke very good English. During a visit to meet him, I happened to mention that I would really like a Harris Tweed jacket, which I had found due to rationing and shortages, was completely unobtainable in Britain. For security reasons we were never given any advance notice of any of our sorties or when we would be sent to different destinations, this information was all based on a need to know basis only. However, my tailor told me with great confidence that I would shortly be leaving to fly to RAF Fayid that was very close to a town called Ismailia. He told me there was a fabric shop in Ismailia where I would be able to purchase some Harris Tweed that he could then use to make me a jacket. I told him I had no idea about which places

I would fly to or indeed when I would be back. He looked at me as though I was quite stupid, as he had clearly just told me. I couldn't help but be amazed, but also a little concerned that my tailor knew my complete itinerary long before I did. A few days later, we were called into the briefing room and given our instructions to fly to RAF Fayid.

My Harris Tweed sports jacket was complete and ready to wear only a week after my initial enquiry, with me having flown to RAF Fayid, been on a shopping trip to Ismailia and then flown my material back across the Western Desert to my tailor. Then only 24 hours after landing back in RAF Shallufa, I was wearing it. I treasured that jacket, not just because of its quality, style and tailoring, but also because of all the memories associated with it.

A few days later we were packing our bags again, this time we were being sent to an RAF base in the Sudan next to the capital city of Khartoum. What a stunning flight that was. From our altitude you could see the Red Sea out on our port side and the River Nile out on our starboard. The journey started over huge expanses of desert, but became slightly more interspersed with a bit of greenery as we went further south. It was very interesting to see large groups of wild gazelle and antelope peacefully grazing until the noise of our aircraft made them scatter in all directions. Lake Nasser, which is on the Egyptian border with the Sudan and fed by the Nile, was spectacular.

The RAF station at Khartoum airport was situated near

the lovely Nile Valley. Our comfortable accommodation was beautiful, but it was so humid that we all ended up pulling our bedding out onto the veranda and sleeping outside under the stars. Sleeping outside, we noticed that the RAF station was heavily protected by armed guards.

It was most apparent that Sudan, like Egypt and the surrounding countries, was also experiencing considerable civil unrest. However, we were allowed to leave the RAF station and go exploring around the fantastic capital city of Khartoum. We came across the statue of General Charles George Gordon sitting astride a camel. Charles Gordon was born in Woolwich, London. I couldn't help but wonder at such things; I'm sure as a small boy growing up in England that no one imagined that many years later there would be a statue of him in the centre of Khartoum. General Gordon was the Governor General of the Sudan for many years. I found out that the statue was later removed in 1958 after the Sudan was granted full independence and shipped back to Britain where it now resides at Gordon's School near Woking, Surrey. The school was founded in 1885 by public subscription as a national memorial to Gordon of Khartoum, suggested by Queen Victoria who became the school's first patron. A member of the royal family has been a patron of the school ever since.

During one of our trips into the capital city, we visited a large open-air street market situated in Omdurman on the outskirts of Khartoum. A couple of us had managed to learn a few words of Arabic and so were able to have a bit of fun haggling. All

I can remember now is "*Bekam di?*" (how much?), "*Shufti?*" (can I have a look?), "*Naaam*" (Yes), "*Laa*" (No) and "*Meshy, halas*", which you said when you shook hands to agree a price. Using our very limited vocabulary we managed to purchase a few souvenirs to take home.

The next few days were spent on flying sorties taking aerial photographs, then a few days off before we flew back to Britain on 20th December 1947, just in time for Christmas.

CHAPTER 27

BERLIN UNDER SIEGE

During January 1948, my commanding officer asked me if I would like to go on a Physical Training instructor's course, as there was a shortage of PT instructors in the RAF. It was an obvious choice for me with all my boxing experience and I knew I would enjoy it.

The course took place at the RAF School of Physical Training in Cosford, situated in Shropshire's very quiet countryside. We had an excellent coach with a gymnastic background. I can remember walking back from a PT session in the park and crossing over a stone bridge with a wall on either side. In mid conversation our coach leapt up onto the wall, did a handstand and then proceeded to walk on his hands all the way along the bridge wall. I remember looking down at the drop into the water below and thinking, "you're on your own there my friend!"

The course was very thorough, covering every aspect of

physical training: running, swimming, refereeing, all kinds of sports and first aid. Our lectures covered all the benefits of the training apparatus and the many ways in which people may injure themselves if they did not use the equipment correctly. I passed my course with very good grades and was awarded all my certificates for the various subjects and my PT Coaching Certificate.

On my return to RAF Wyton I was given a training schedule that involved three days a week coaching various aircrew members. Most crew members were already quite fit, so all I had to do was give them a training routine and enable them to get the most from the equipment they used. I had just settled into this routine when our crew were informed that we were required to go back out to Egypt again. It had been fabulous spending so much time with Barbara, but I had expected to be sent back out to Egypt or the Sudan at some point, due to the problems and unrest that still existed there.

We set off on 1st March 1948 and had the normal stopover at Castel Benito, Libya, before continuing our journey out to Shallufa. As soon as we arrived back in Egypt we were kept very busy for the next twenty days, flying almost every day on air to ground firing. It was on one of these occasions that we had a rather nasty prang on landing. The aircraft overshot the runway and came to a sudden halt in the sand. We were all thrown about in the back; I hit my head badly and felt a bit dazed for a few minutes and the rest of the crew all had bumps and bruises although fortunately no one was seriously injured. It was a stark reminder though that flying was always fraught with danger - everything from the weather, pilot error, navigation errors or mechanical failures.

We were given a couple of days off to recover while both we and our aircraft were repaired for minor damage, but we were all soon back flying again. Our next sortie was to fly to RAF Habbiniya, the RAF headquarters in Iraq, situated west of the Euphrates. RAF Habbiniya was a large airport and aircraft depot, surrounded by over seven miles of perimeter fencing. The crew facilities at RAF Habbiniya were incredible; we had never seen anything like it. There were numerous tennis courts, rugby, football and hockey pitches, a golf course, riding stables, gymnasium, a swimming pool, both an indoor as well as an outdoor cinema and a church. There were mooring facilities for yachts and even flying boats and all forms of water sports available. The RAF base was like an oasis in a large desert. We were like kids with a new playground as we made ourselves at home.

Britain had ruled over Iraq after the Turks were defeated at the end of the Mesopotamian Campaign during World War 1. This was a very hot land, a turbulent country populated by a number of different races with tribal factions and sheikhdoms. The one thing that united them was their common purpose of ridding themselves of British rule. Britain was keen to keep

Iraq as it had the second largest oil reserves in the world, having more oil than Europe and South America combined and second only to Saudi Arabia. It wasn't just the desire to keep the oil under British control, but also to ensure that this precious resource didn't fall into "the wrong hands" as British politicians questioned Iraq's ability to be able to hold onto it against other stronger countries if British troops pulled out.

During World War 2, Hitler was keen to obtain the oil fields for Germany, so he used the resistance groups, by sending them ammunition and stirring up anti-British propaganda. In the end, a force of over 45,000 fully trained and equipped Iraqi military personnel rose against the British, but they were defeated after weeks of bloodshed. The British military forces were therefore able to protect the Mosul oil wells on which the Allies depended so much during the war.

We returned to Britain on 31st March 1948 and over the next few months I settled back into PT coaching and boxing training. My days off were all spent with Barbara and her family.

Life was very settled until we got notification that we would be flying back out to Egypt, departing on 15th June 1948. From Shallufa we then positioned down to Habbiniya in Iraq. Although we loved the incredible facilities at Habbiniya RAF station we were always very aware of how volatile the situation was in Iraq. We always had to be on our guard when leaving the confines of the RAF station and so therefore mainly stayed on site. For this reason, the RAF allowed a number of trusted tradesmen onto the airfield to set up stalls, as a small on-site market. A couple of RAF personnel highly recommended a silversmith craftsman jeweller who regularly visited the base, so next time he was on site I sought him out and asked him to make a silver and gold bracelet for Barbara. He showed me some items he had made and I chose a style I liked and asked if he could engrave her initials on it for me too - B.R.F (Barbara Rose Ford). I returned about an hour later and he had already finished it ready for me to collect. It was absolutely stunning, made mainly from silver, with some gold decorations. I had been longing to get home to Barbara before, but now I was so excited to see her again and give her this special gift.

On 25th June 1948 we started our return flight back to Britain, stopping off at Castel Benito in Libya and then setting off the next day for home. The flight between Iraq and Libya took us seven hours and the flight from Libya to England took us eight hours 40 minutes.

On our arrival back at base the place was buzzing with rumours and news reports about the high possibility that we might soon be at war with Soviet Russia. Radio and newspapers were stating that war looked inevitable. In response to this, all service personnel were immediately put on high alert, ready for immediate action and all days off and leave were cancelled. I put the bracelet I had bought for Barbara safely away in a locker and wondered how long it would be before I got to see her again.

Soviet Russia had finally decided to rid itself of Western interference and decided the best way to get the French,

British and the US out of Berlin was to put the sectors that they governed under siege. As Berlin was sited right in the middle of Russian controlled Germany, they simply barricaded all approach roads and closed all railway lines into and out of these sections of Berlin. This was an incredibly aggressive manoeuvre and one that in normal circumstances would almost certainly have ignited another war. However, no one wanted, nor could afford World War 3, so the Allies reacted by setting up a daily cargo flight into Berlin carrying in much needed food and commodity supplies, thereby avoiding any direct confrontation with the Russians. Stalin didn't imagine that Britain and the USA would try to fly in supplies as the population requiring feeding was so huge. No one wanted to back down, but no one wanted a war either. The cargo planes delivering the daily supplies of food and other essentials were regularly buzzed by Russian MiG fighter aircraft. They were very threatening but they held back from attack as the Russians knew that there were US bomber aircraft, armed with nuclear bombs, based in Britain, ready to scramble.

Stalin did not have nuclear weaponry, at this point, so this worked as a huge deterrent.

Russia's blockade tactic carried on for nearly twelve months, with both sides flexing their muscles at each another, but thankfully managing not to let it escalate into a war. Finally, on 12th May 1949, Stalin lifted the blockade, but the race to gather atomic weaponry increased in Soviet Russia and by August 1949 Stalin had tested his first atomic warhead.

At first, we were on full readiness to be deployed out to Germany in case things developed, and all days off and leave were cancelled, but six weeks into the blockade I did manage to get a few days off and immediately set off to Barbara's house. It was wonderful to pull up outside her house. It had been about two months since I last saw her and we hadn't been able to even send a letter to one another. I just hoped she was home. I had just got out of the car when I heard one of the twins shouting excitedly for Barbara and she came rushing out of the house and straight into my arms. I lived for these moments and the wonderful warm welcome I received from all her family. It was also the first opportunity I had to give Barbara the bracelet I had commissioned to be made whilst out in Iraq. Stalin's blockade had delayed me getting it to her, but she could not have been more delighted to receive it. As I said to her, I doubted that there could be many girls in Britain, let alone in West Row, with a bracelet made out in Iraq. She was thrilled with it and we just had such a happy time catching up with one another's news.

On 10th September 1948 our crew was called in for a special briefing by our commanding officer, where we were informed, much to our immense delight that we had been selected to perform the Battle of Britain Flypast over Buckingham Palace. We were being sent to make a practice run later that day.

Every year since the war ended, there has been an annual celebration called Battle of Britain Day which is celebrated on 15th September. This battle was the first major battle carried out entirely by two enemy air forces, the German Luftwaffe and the British Royal Air Force. Battle of Britain Day is always commemorated by an RAF flypast over Buckingham Palace.

It was a huge honour to be selected to be part of this occasion and we were informed that we would be carrying Richard Dimbleby as a passenger, who would be broadcasting live from our aircraft on national radio throughout the flypast. Richard Dimbleby, dubbed "the voice of the nation", was a famous war correspondent and the BBC's commentator on all royal and state occasions. He was of course, father to both David and Johnathan Dimbleby, who went on to become equally famous for their roles as television and radio presenters in political and current affairs.

Richard Dimbleby's full commentary, from take-off to landing, went live to the nation. To his credit, in order to properly view the entire proceedings, he stood throughout the whole flight, three hours and 10 minutes, holding on to the back of the pilot's seat. The aircraft was a Lincoln bomber, registration LS D piloted by Flt Lt Scott.

On 10th November 1948 we flew back out to Shallufa, returning nine days later. We arrived back on 19th November 1948, just in time for the RAF boxing championships on 20th November 1948, held at RAF Wakefield. I was delighted to win the RAF Bomber Command Middleweight Championship again that year.

To celebrate, a group of us from the base decided to treat ourselves to a day at the races. As we walked towards the betting stands we were greeted by a tall, very colourful dark skinned man with a broad, beaming, smiling face and gold fillings in his teeth. He was wearing coloured pantaloons, a crisp white shirt and a huge feathered headdress. We soon found out he was a showman, known as Prince Monolulu, a flamboyant national celebrity who attended racing events all over the country as well as open-air markets, and other gatherings, particularly in London.

He was the type of person you immediately warmed to, but was clearly a bit of a con man too, but you just couldn't help but like and admire him. He stood amongst the crowds shouting: "I've gotta *horse, I've* gotta *horse!*" and for a few pence would hand out a hot tip telling you which horse you should bet on in the next race. To test Prince Monolulu, three of us bought a tip from him at different times. He'd given us all three different horses, so his plan was that if he told different people different horses at least some people in the crowd would win and return to give him a thank you tip from part of their winnings. It made us chuckle as we saw him happily accepting thank you tips throughout the duration of the racing schedule. He would make a big fuss of those who tipped him, which had two positive effects; firstly, others could see his racing knowledge was worth having and secondly it encouraged the next set of winners to give him a small share of their winnings too. Such a simple trick, but it only worked because of his flamboyant personality. Post-war Britain needed joyous colourful characters like Prince Monolulu to cheer its people up and make them live and laugh a little once again.

CHAPTER 28

OUR WEDDING DAY

We decided to get married on New Year's Day 1949, as we thought it would be the best possible way to start the New Year - as a married couple. I already had ten days leave booked for the New Year and I managed to arrange some leave in early December, in order that we could sort out our wedding plans. The date was agreed by Barbara's parents, who said they would be able to make all the necessary arrangements and we wrote to my parents to give them as much notice as possible, as despite the distance I knew they would want to be there if they could.

My leave in early December was spent wedding planning with Barbara's family. We had a wonderful time and we were all so excited. Barbara and I had an appointment to see the vicar of

St Mary's Church in Mildenhall to sort out the formalities and we attended church in order to hear our banns being read out. Barbara and her family often went to West Row Church, but at the time it wasn't used for weddings, as Mildenhall was the main church in the diocese.

I can still remember how excited I was on New Year's Eve when I drove to Mildenhall railway station to collect my parents and my brother Herbert. I had made bookings for my family and I to stay at the Bell Hotel in Mildenhall, which was just opposite the church.

Unfortunately, my sister Cis couldn't come as she was now with her husband out in the USA. It was fabulous to see the rest of my family though. Bert and I sat downstairs in the hotel for hours catching up on one another's news. I had asked him to be my best man and he wanted to run through his speech with me. He then explained that he was due to go to a fancy-dress party when he got home and hadn't had time to find a fancy-dress outfit yet. I knew that there was a very good fancy-dress shop in Cambridge, so I suggested that we got up early, caught a train and then rushed back in time for the wedding. We didn't have time to tell our family, as we were up and out, before anyone else had stirred. The only fancy-dress item we could find which fitted Bert, was a pageboy outfit, which he quickly purchased, and then we set off, at a run, through the streets of Cambridge, back to the railway station. We knew we were tight on time, but as we arrived, we were horrified to see the platform attendant closing the platform gate, as our train was now gathering steam ready to leave the station. If we missed this train, we would miss the wedding, so we both pushed our way past the guard and leapt over the platform gate, with him yelling after us. I grabbed the carriage door handle just as the train started pulling away and we both threw ourselves into the carriage, puffing, panting and laughing with relief. As we sank back into our seats, I think there was more steam coming off us than the train! When I look back now, I can't believe I put my wedding day plans in such jeopardy just to find a fancy-dress costume for my brother, but it seemed totally reasonable to us at the time. It was just so nice to spend some quality time with my brother.

The wedding was at 2pm and as we chugged out of the station in Cambridge it was already 11am. The train seemed to take an eternity to gain a reasonable speed, as the fireman added more coal. I had just started to relax, feeling that we were finally on our way, when the driver started to apply the brakes. It was then that I remembered that the local people always laughingly referred to this particular train service as the "Mildenhall *Express*", as not only was it a slow train, but worse still, it stopped at various farms along the route. Our first stop was a farmer's field in the middle of nowhere. Once the train had come to a standstill, the guard slowly and carefully lowered the steps from the front carriage to allow two people to board the train. Once they were safely on board, the guard then took his time carefully stowing the steps again. Once he was satisfied that all was in order, he waved his flag so that the train driver could continue the journey. The train then slowly rattled along gradually gathering speed, but the second we reached a decent pace, we started the whole painstakingly slow process all over again as we stopped to pick up an elderly farmer a few fields further along. The elderly man required assistance to board the train and was enjoying a very lengthy slow conversation with the guard as he did it. I could barely contain my impatience. I'm sure it would have been quicker to jog home, but it was a long way between Cambridge and Mildenhall.

On the train journey back to Mildenhall, Herbert confided in me that he was seriously considering emigrating to Malta, a country that had been recommended to him by some friends who had served there during the war. I was absolutely stunned, but had to agree that it was a beautiful country. I had flown into Luqa Airfield in Malta on 18th November 1948 on our way back to England from Egypt. We normally landed at Castel Benito Airfield in Libya, but there was a lot of civil unrest in Libya at the time, so we had been directed to use Malta as a refuelling point instead.

As we slowly rattled our way along the tracks, stopping to pick up people from what seemed like every field, my mind strayed back to Malta. I could understand Bert's friends persuading him to emigrate there; it was a beautiful island. I remembered circling around the airport waiting to land and looking down at the beautiful sheltered harbour and the capital city of Valletta. It was a stunning city that reminded me of Venice. Sadly, you could see some damage caused by enemy bombing raids, but the majesty of the city was still breath-taking. I had heard that Malta was a very devout religious nation and certainly as your eye scanned the view below you could clearly see a multitude of church spires and domes. There are at least 25 churches in Valletta alone and over 313 churches on the island in total, with another 46 churches on the island of Gozo, four of which are magnificent cathedrals. I fell in love with this beautiful Mediterranean island in those brief minutes as we circled overhead.

On landing in Luqa it was clear that we were very definitely on extremely friendly Allied soil. Our welcome was second to none and in stark contrast to the reception and tension we felt whenever we spent any time in Libya.

Malta had been part of the British Empire since 1800, and had always been looked upon as a highly prized military and naval fortress. Malta's position in the Mediterranean Sea made it an ideal military location during World War 2 and as such the Germans and Italians were determined to destroy or conquer Malta. As a result, in the early stages of World War 2 Malta took a considerable battering. It was under siege with virtually no cargo ships managing to reach its ports through constant attack from enemy aircraft. Despite this, the Maltese spirit held out and still stayed loyal to Britain and the Allies. In recognition of its bravery, devotion and heroism King George VI awarded the Island of Malta the George Cross by Royal Warrant in a letter to the Governor-General Lieutenant General Dobbie on 15th April 1942.

I had heard a number of RAF personnel who had been stationed in Malta say that if they survived the war, they fancied emigrating there. The main reasons given were that they enjoyed the climate and the beauty of the island, and because they respected and admired the Maltese people.

My brother was delighted to hear all the information and anecdotes I could provide about Malta. I told him all about its pretty roadside cafés. I recalled being asked by a waiter if I wanted a slice of fresh lemon in my drink, which I did; in response the waiter simply reached up into the tree next to the café, plucked a lemon, cut me a slice and popped it into my drink. Whenever I am offered a slice of fresh lemon I often think back to that moment.

To pass the time during our journey, I also told Bert all about the RAF boys who had unlawfully taken a train to get themselves back to Mildenhall base one night. When I had first arrived at RAF Mildenhall, everyone on the station had been confined to barracks until someone owned up to being responsible for the train incident. The confinement was short-lived as the culprits come forward the next day. Apparently, a number of aircrew had travelled by train from Mildenhall into Cambridge to have a much-deserved night out, having completed a tour of operations. They had a fantastic evening and then returned to Cambridge railway station to discover that the last train had left. There was a steam train parked in the station ready for the first trip in the morning, but the platform gates were closed and the train was all shut down. One of the aircrew had been a train driver before enlisting. Encouraged by his associates, and with the help of one of them who had volunteered to be the stoker, they got the train going and took it all the way back to Mildenhall railway station and abandoned it there. It was a huge scandal.

My mother was waiting outside the hotel looking for us when we came rushing around the corner into view. She didn't delay us by asking questions but told us both to hurry and get ourselves ready. I ran up the stairs, to my room and quickly changed into my suit. I could have chosen to get married in my RAF uniform, but instead I chose to wear a morning suit, which I had hired. Thankfully, I had left everything laid out ready to put on, so quickly changed and then dashed back downstairs to join my family who were already dressed and ready to leave for the church.

The only person missing from the wedding party now was Herbert who took longer to get ready than me. I was standing chatting to my dad when the whole room fell silent and my parents' faces dropped in horror. I turned to follow their stunned gaze and saw Herbert happily descending the stairs dressed in his fancy-dress pageboy outfit, announcing that he was now ready to go. No one knew about our early morning quest to Cambridge to find the outfit and they all thought he was serious. After a period of stunned silence my father managed to find his voice saying: "If you think I've come all this bloody way to be shown up by you, you have another think coming." My poor father never swore, but the spectacle of Herbert dressed in his pageboy outfit and thinking of him standing as the best man at the head of the aisle was all too much for my father. Long after Herbert had explained it was all a joke and even once Herbert had changed, my father was still muttering about it. The hotel staff and other guests who witnessed it found it hilarious and I was still chuckling as Herbert and I sat in the church waiting for Barbara to arrive. We didn't have long to wait, as Barbara was her usual impeccably punctual self. As the clock started to strike 2pm, Barbara entered the church and the organ started to play *Here comes the Bride*. I immediately sprung to my feet and turned around to see my beautiful bride walking towards me down the aisle. She took my breath away.

We said our vows to one another surrounded by the loving embrace of our families and closest friends in Mildenhall's majestic 16th-century church, and so started my life as a very happy and contented married man. Our marriage has lasted over seventy-one years. Barbara is the love of my life and my very best friend and still the most beautiful woman I have ever known.

After the service the wedding party and guests all travelled over to West Row village hall, which was not far from the River Lark where we had first met over three years before, under a weeping willow tree.

When we entered the village hall, I was astounded to see a beautiful three-tier wedding cake taking centre stage in the hall. Rationing meant that it was almost impossible to get the ingredients for a cake, especially for a large three-tier wedding

Our wedding day, 1st January 1949,
St Mary's Church in Mildenhall.

Our three-tier wedding cake!

Barbara on our honeymoon, in London.

Barbara on our honeymoon, in London.

cake, fully iced and decorated. I was as surprised and delighted as all of our guests. Barbara explained that her parents had a family friend Elsie who, with her husband, owned a large, lucrative pub in the West End of London and it was they who had managed to source the cake for us. Barbara's brother Gerald worked for them and so brought the cake back with him the day before the wedding. Barbara had been as amazed as we were to find that it wasn't just one small cake, but a stunning three-tier cake. Elsie couldn't take time off to attend the wedding, but was determined to be part of our special day. She sent a lovely wedding card saying she hoped we enjoyed the cake and apologising that it was sponge rather than fruitcake, as the ingredients for a fruitcake were impossible to source. She also said she'd sent a special wedding gift just for Barbara, which Gerald also had in the car with him.

Barbara was so excited when she opened it - Elsie had been so thoughtful and sent Barbara a beautiful, navy blue, fitted, jersey dress. Clothes were impossible to buy due to rationing and there was very little choice in Mildenhall. We had planned to stay in London for our honeymoon and although Barbara was extremely excited to be going, she was also equally fretful about what to wear, as she felt everything she owned looked too worn, too old fashioned or too young on her now. What a kind and thoughtful gift this was and what a difference it made to Barbara as she packed for our honeymoon away.

All too soon the festivities and the cake were all finished and it was time to say our farewells, as we set off on our first adventure together as a married couple. Russell Palmer was our local taxi driver and it was he who drove Barbara and her father to the church and then drove Barbara and myself to the reception. He then returned later to pick us up and drive us to Mildenhall railway station. We stopped briefly at Barbara's parents' house, for her to get changed into her beautiful new blue dress. Her wedding dress had been hired from a store in London, so her parents were going to post it back for her. Russell then drove us to the train station and wished us a fantastic honeymoon. We caught the train from Mildenhall to Cambridge and then from Cambridge to Charing Cross. We were lucky to get a single compartment to ourselves all the way to London. We then caught a taxi from Charing Cross station to the Queens Park Hotel where we were staying for our honeymoon - for one whole glorious week.

After arriving at the hotel we went for an evening stroll and noticed that *Cinderella* starring, Tommy Trinder, was being performed at the London Palladium Theatre in Argyll Street. All the seats were taken, but there were standing room only tickets still available so we took those.

Despite the discomfort of having to stand throughout the performance, we thoroughly enjoyed it. The principal actors were Tommy Trinder as Buttons, Evelyn Laye as Cinderella and two American comedians, George and Bert Bernard as the two ugly sisters. Some years later, I was introduced to Tommy Trinder at a party where he was the guest of honour. He was a most friendly and sociable man and I obtained his autograph to give to my young son.

It was a fabulous performance. On leaving the theatre we joined a small queue of people who like ourselves had been drawn to the lovely smell of roasted chestnuts that were being sold for a few pence from a small transportable barbecue, which the vendor pushed along the street. We took them up to our bedroom in the hotel and sat down in front of the gas fire in our room.

The weather was very good for this time of year, so we spent many happy hours enjoying all the sights of London. On Sunday morning we watched the speakers at Hyde Park Corner. Informal speakers would stand on soapboxes as improvised platforms, talking about different subjects including religion and politics; a few would attract a small audience from passers by. In 1872 an act had been passed allowing anyone to speak publicly at Hyde Park Corner on a Sunday and discuss any subject they wanted. Some of the famous speakers have included Karl Marx, Vladimir Lenin and George Orwell.

Whilst in Hyde Park we also saw several people out exercising their horses. From there we went to Kensington Gardens to see the memorial of Prince Albert, the Prince Consort of Queen Victoria who was born and raised at Kensington Palace. She had the memorial built there in remembrance of her husband who died of typhoid in 1861.

The next day we took a stroll around Green Park. We didn't know it then, but sixty-three years later we would have the privilege of being invited to Green Park to see HRH Queen Elizabeth II unveil the Bomber Command Memorial.

Barbara particularly wanted to visit the British Museum where the Mildenhall Roman Treasure trove is kept. Barbara's uncle, Sydney Ford, was a farmer and an agricultural engineer, with land in West Row and the Fens. In January 1942 his ploughman returned early explaining that he had just dug up a large black metal object. The two men went back out to the field with some shovels and in the freshly ploughed land managed to unearth 34 of these black metal objects. Sydney took them home, washed and polished them and they cleaned up beautifully. There were silver dishes, bowls, a large silver tray, goblets and spoons. Research revealed that these items must have been buried by the Romans during the fourth century AD when they had occupied parts of England. West Row has always had rich pastureland, particularly good for breeding sheep, and was occupied by some very wealthy Romans. As the Romans began to lose their control of Britain, there were lots of uprisings and many Roman properties were attacked and pillaged. To protect their treasured items, many families buried their most valuable items in the hope of retrieving them when law and order was restored.

Sydney hadn't realised that he needed to notify the authorities of the find and so had kept the silver in the house for four years until a local doctor saw some of the items displayed around the house and explained what he needed to do. Barbara is still amazed that she used to handle such rare objects. The large embossed silver tray, approximately sixty centimetres (two feet) in diameter, which has been named "The Great Plate of

Bacchus", was kept behind her uncle's sofa and the children used to pull it out and hit it with their hand as it made a lovely gong.

Having finally been handed over to the correct authorities, a court decided on 1st July 1946 that these silver objects were in fact treasure trove and they became the property of the Crown. Had they been handed in immediately the family would have been given a substantial reward, but because they had kept them for so long, they only received £2000 to be shared between Sydney and his ploughman Gordon Butcher. Barbara was delighted to visit the museum and see the Mildenhall Treasure in all its glory.

All too soon our honeymoon came to an end and we returned home to West Row. We could have opted to have married quarters at RAF Wyton, but as I was often away from base, we decided it was best for Barbara to return home and live with her parents and for me to go and stay when I had days off. I was kept extremely busy on my return to base, so I was very pleased that Barbara was back home with her family.

Our son, John David Meller.

CHAPTER 29

BABY BOOM

RAF personnel were being demobbed daily and so flight crews were being trained to undertake maintenance and repair work on some of the aircraft systems. I had previous experience working at Burtonwood on aircraft electrical systems so I was selected for training and certified to service the electrical equipment on Lincoln bombers. I was also sent on courses to qualify me to drive various types of RAF vehicles and machinery too.

Clothes rationing ended on 15th of March 1949. It didn't affect me greatly as I was still mainly in uniform, but I can remember the excitement of Barbara, her mother Rose and the twins, Pat and Pam as they were now allowed to buy as many items of clothing as they wanted, but for some considerable time afterwards clothing was still very hard to obtain.

Food was still strictly rationed, and in some ways this seemed to be a good thing as you rarely, if ever, saw anybody who looked even remotely overweight. Whilst there were cases of hardship the nation as a whole looked very fit and healthy.

It was in March 1949 that Barbara gave me the exciting news that she was expecting our first child. We could hardly contain our excitement and I sat down immediately to write to my family to let them know. I could only imagine my mother's face when she finally received my letter. The period from 1946 to 1964 became known as the "Baby Boom", as there was a noticeable increase in births during these years.

Barbara and I would often go away for short break holidays on my days off. We would pack everything into my MG sports car and set off on another short adventure.

My life was busy and extremely full. I was a newly married man with a baby on the way, an aircrew member, fitness trainer, driver, aircraft electrical engineer and I was still busy with my boxing too.

I was a middleweight boxer, which was by far the biggest category. Later this was split into light middleweight and middleweight, but when I was competing it was just one big category and hugely competitive. You had so many fights to contend, the moment you won a fight you literally clambered out of that ring and went straight into the next.

I was selected for an exhibition bout in British occupied Berlin. It was very interesting returning four years after the war.

I was astounded by the difference, both in the regeneration of the city and its people. It was great to receive many friendly handshakes from the Germans and also see the two nationalities working side by side with mutual respect for each other to rejuvenate this section of the capital city.

There was good news at the beginning of April 1949 as I was told that my transfer to Mildenhall had been approved, which meant that I could finally live at home with Barbara and her family full time. I completed my final flight from RAF Wyton on 20th April and was given a couple of days leave in order to be able to relocate. It was almost five years since I had lived in a family environment. Barbara's home was so welcoming and full of fun and love. Rose kept the house immaculate and it always looked well furnished and decorated; yet due to furniture rations Rose, like many householders had managed to improvise. For instance, our bedside tables were recycled orange boxes standing on their sides, there was a divide in the middle of the box to stop the oranges rolling around which made a perfect shelf. Rose had fitted a small curtain to the front and put a material runner over the top. They looked very pretty and cottagey, but were also very functional.

World politics and unrest were calming down and there appeared to be an easing of relations between Soviet Russia and the West with the lifting of the blockade of Berlin, but the Cold War still continued. The runways at RAF Mildenhall were in the process of being extended yet again, to accommodate the US WB-50 Superfortress aircraft. The USA wanted Soviet Russia to see that they still had a major force in Britain, on standby, ready for action. Our combat flying training still continued too with operations Polka Dot, Ding Dong and various squadron exercises.

It was about this time I decided to change my MG sports car and buy something much more practical as a family vehicle. I went for a beautiful saloon car that was manufactured by AJS motorcycles. This car was one of only a few made for the firm's company directors, so it was an extremely rare model. I loved this vehicle, as it was stunning to look at, very comfortable and easy to drive, but sadly I didn't keep it for long as it was impossible to get spare parts to fit, so I sold it to another aircrew member whose father was a car mechanic. They gave me a good price for it as they were delighted to have this very rare collector's car.

Considering I was the one who flew into combat, Barbara always seemed to be the one who had close calls. One evening in May 1949, Barbara, who was now five months pregnant, and I were taking a leisurely walk along the banks of the River Lark and were reminiscing about our first meeting under the weeping willow tree, when Barbara suddenly jumped back quickly as she almost trod on something moving under her feet. It was a fairly large snake with dark zigzag lines running down the length of its spine and an inverted V on its neck. We both realised that it was an adder, a venomous snake native to Britain, which can grow up to three feet long. Adders are not particularly aggressive and only use their venom as a last means of defence, but I'm pretty certain it would have used its venom if trodden on. As we watched the adder retreat, we both realised how lucky Barbara had been to react like she did, for had she been bitten I dread to think what the outcome might have been to both her and our unborn baby.

On 24th September 1949 Barbara woke me up in the early hours of the morning as she had gone into labour, she was ten days early, but was certain she needed to get to hospital as soon as she could. I told her parents and then rushed Barbara to Newmarket Hospital. I was due to report for duty soon and scheduled to fly later that morning. The midwife reassured me that she would take very good care of my wife and that my services would not be needed. I hated to leave Barbara there, but they clearly didn't want me in their way. It was difficult driving away and my thoughts were entirely with Barbara throughout that flight. I was so relieved when we landed; the rest of the crew knew my impatience to get away so helped in every way they could. As soon as I was able, I dashed to the nearest public telephone box, rang the hospital and was informed that Barbara had just given birth to a healthy baby boy. They promised to let her know that I had phoned and to inform her that I was just leaving RAF Mildenhall and would be with her very shortly. I couldn't believe it – we were now a family. I couldn't wait to hold my son and see my amazing wife.

CHAPTER 30

DEMOB

The arrival of our baby son, whom we named John David, changed everything. I loved my parents-in-law's home, but as our son began to grow into a toddler, it was clear that we now needed a home of our own. We couldn't afford a home on my RAF salary and we didn't want to move into married quarters, as I wasn't planning to stay in the RAF as a long-term career, so I decided that it was time to consider a new profession.

I was acutely aware that thousands of service personnel were being demobilised all the time and over one million people had recently been released from munitions and weaponry factories, so I was expecting it to be difficult to secure a suitable job, with sufficient salary to make it viable for me to leave the RAF.

I was therefore shocked at the speed with which my demob occurred. For some reason, that I still cannot explain, I sent my curriculum vitae to the Metropolitan Police Force in London, and very quickly received a written reply inviting me for an interview at Peel House, Regency Street in London. My interview went well and so within a short while I found myself signed up for my new career and a whole new life in London.

It was during my police interview that I realised just how much life experience and qualifications I, and other young men like myself, who had survived the war without serious injury, had to offer. Our life experiences of travel, comradeship, combat, first aid, survival skills, PT instruction, languages, geography, electronics and engineering meant that most of us were highly sought after in various careers. It made me realise how very different my life would have been had the war not occurred. I would most likely have spent my whole life living and working within a narrow radius from where I was born and most significantly, I certainly would never have met and married Barbara.

On 13th March 1950, aged 25 years, I officially started my new career as a trainee police constable in the Metropolitan Police at the police training college in Hendon, London.

I was ready to leave, but it still felt strange walking out from the gates of RAF Mildenhall dressed as a civilian. I had been issued with a demob suit, which consisted of a trilby hat, a jacket, a waistcoat, one set of trousers, one white shirt, a tie, socks, shoes, a suitcase, food coupons and a Discharge Reference Book. I was given a period of leave during March, called demob leave which meant I would still get my pay from the RAF to help tide me over until I was receiving my new salary as a police officer.

Returning to civilian life was a poignant moment. I had been part of Great Britain's mighty fighting force and had been there during its "Greatest Hour". I found it a little ironic that "Great Britain", which had commenced the 20th century with the most extensive empire the world had ever known, managed to lose her prefix "Great" at the point when she had never deserved that accolade more.

I knew I would miss my life in the RAF. I had spent every day of adulthood in active service. I was aware that conflicts were still rife around the globe and that due to human nature warfare would always be a threat. The Cold War with Soviet Russia could escalate at any time and if it did, a state of emergency would be declared and I knew that I would immediately be called up again, but for now, at least, I had played my part and my wife and our young son were now my main concern. However, for the next ten years I did volunteer for the RAF Reserve.

As I walked away contemplating the exciting time ahead of me with my wonderful wife, my beautiful baby son, my new career and the new adventure of living in London, I felt a huge weight of sadness for all my lost colleagues who would never know this moment. So many of my friends had not lived to enjoy the glory of our victory. I was only too aware that I was only able to set off on the next chapter of my life, because they had sacrificed theirs. I honoured them in my thoughts as I ventured forth.

Although my life moved on, I still wanted to keep a link with my RAF past and with my fallen comrades. Barbara and I were privileged to be able to visit Mildenhall air force base once a year, to attend an annual reunion of RAF service personnel who had previously been stationed there. We really enjoyed these reunion meals and went fairly regularly over the years. The Mildenhall "Roll of Honour" records the names of 1,900 aircrew killed on active service with some of these airmen being buried in a well-maintained Military Cemetery at the back of St Johns Church in the adjacent village of Beck Row and some buried in the cemetery in West Row. Barbara's great grandfather Leonard Ellington, was the Parson at West Row Chapel for many years and so Barbara and her family had a strong tie to this church and often attended services there.

Barbara and I also became very active members of SSAFA (the Soldiers, Sailors and Air Force Association) and in 1993 we were both invited to see the unveiling of the Battle of Britain Memorial by HRH Queen Elizabeth, the Queen Mother, at Capel-le-Ferne (situated between Folkestone and Dover), high on the cliffs overlooking the English Channel which was the scene of many aerial combats during the Battle of Britain. Memorials are very important to those who grieve and remember. There was a sadness that whilst several memorials existed to commemorate RAF personnel in general, there was no memorial specific to Bomber Command, in remembrance and recognition of the 55,573 Bomber Command aircrew members who lost their lives during World War 2.

Finally, on 4th May 2011, the Foundation Stone for the long awaited Bomber Command Memorial was laid by HRH The Duke of Gloucester in Green Park, London in the presence of Marshal of the Royal Air Force Sir Michael Beetham, President of the Bomber Command Association. The songwriter and singer Robin Gibb, (from the band the Bee Gees) was hugely instrumental in raising funds for the memorial and driving the project through to completion. Robin was struck by the huge injustice for the young aircrew and their families, who had paid the ultimate price following orders and defending their country, but had not received a fitting accolade due to the sensitivity over the extensive damage caused by Bomber Command to German cities.

The devastation and death caused by Bomber Command is of immense sorrow, but the Nazi regime was the cause, all other actions by both sides were sadly just the result. Our military leaders were simply responding in any way they could to break that regime. The 55,573 men who lost their lives following orders and protecting their country and Europe need to be remembered and honoured. They were all volunteers with an average age of 22 years, who signed up knowing they faced some of the worst odds of survival in World War 2. For every five men who volunteered as Bomber Command aircrew, three would fail to complete a tour of duty with many being killed in action on their first operation. This memorial was sixty-five years overdue. It is rather fitting that Robin Gibb, the songwriter who wrote the song *Staying Alive,* helped to keep the memory of so many war heroes alive forever too. It was of great sadness that Robin Gibb lost his fight against cancer and died just one month before the unveiling of the memorial.

On 28th June 2012 Barbara and I, our son John David and his wife Christine, our daughter Caroline and her husband Jamie and their daughter Stephanie were all invited to attend the unveiling ceremony for this magnificent monument. It was indeed an incredible weekend to remember, bringing back a flood of memories. I was very touched and humbled to find that London cab drivers refused to take payment for transporting any veteran to and from the Memorial Day service that day. My taxi driver just looked me in the eye and said: "No sir, it is me who needs to say thank you- to you".

My family, along with over 6,000 other veterans, widows and their families all gathered to witness the unveiling conducted by Her Majesty the Queen.

We were all in awe of the bronze monument that had been sculptured by Philip Jackson. The life-size bronze statue depicts a seven-man bomber crew having just returned from operational combat. Five of them are looking up scanning the sky, in hope and desperation for the return of other aircraft and their crews, two of the figures are looking down, reflecting on the horror they have just endured. The attention to detail in their uniform and equipment is fabulous. The statue evokes so much emotion, empathy and memories, and has truly captured a moment in history, which any World War 2 Bomber Command aircrew can relate to.

The unveiling of the memorial was blessed with glorious sunshine. On arrival we were all ushered to our seats by members of both the Royal Air Force University Squadron and Air Training Corp (ATC Cadets) who had travelled from different parts of Britain to give every assistance to the veterans and their families on this very special day. They were all incredibly attentive and were kept very busy handing out thousands of bottles of water, due to the heat of the day. These very polite, caring youngsters were indeed a great credit to the youth of our country. There were also a large number of volunteer helpers from the RAF Benevolent Fund charity. The whole atmosphere was incredible and we were so grateful for all those who had worked to make this event such a momentous occasion.

It was a pleasure to see so many veterans, wartime widows and their families, a number of whom had travelled from New Zealand, Canada, Australia and the USA and other countries throughout the Commonwealth.

John Sargent and Carol Vorderman MBE were on the stage, but also circulated amongst the audience talking to veterans about their experiences. The music that had been selected was very moving and included: *Abide with me; Bring Him Home; Here's to the Heroes; Nessun Dorma; Hallelujah* and *Jerusalem*. The speeches and the singing of the choirs could not have been better. We were a very large audience, but we all sat spellbound and greatly touched by this incredible tribute.

The RAF provided a flypast of five Tornados in a "V" formation. This was followed by the incredible sight of a Lancaster bomber which dropped thousands of poppies over Green Park where we were all seated. The ATC and RAF Cadets busied themselves collecting the fallen poppies and handing them out as keepsakes to all the veterans and their families. Seeing this aircraft and hearing the roar of those four Merlin engines brought back so many memories for both me and Barbara and brought a lump to our throats as we both squeezed each other's hands with emotion.

The Lancaster was flown by Squadron Leader Russell who, when reporting to air traffic control on his radio transmission said:

"We're a Lancaster bomber with ten people on board and 55,573 souls."

One of the ten on board was Squadron Leader Ron Clark DFC, the captain of the original 100 Squadron Phantom of the Ruhr. He had been invited to join the crew and release the poppies from the bomb bay. As he did so he was heard to say "Lest we forget".

After the ceremony, both Her Majesty the Queen and her husband the Duke of Edinburgh, shook hands and spoke to a number of veterans who had travelled from abroad. HRH Prince Charles and the Duchess of Cornwall shook hands and had a short conversation with a number of veterans including myself. Prince Charles also kindly shook hands with Stephanie our granddaughter who was standing next to me.

Letters, photographs and other items of memorabilia were

left on the memorial and collected by one of the officials to be preserved for the future. One of the letters stated: "In loving memory of Monte Shute. Beloved husband of Grace Ethel Parsons, now 91 and still remembering". The official who read her note decided to write to Ethel and arranged to meet her. Ethel showed the officer photographs of Monte and explained that they had only been married for one year when her husband, a navigator, had been killed along with the rest of his crew, when their bomber had been shot down on operations. She expressed how glad she was that finally there was a monument in remembrance of the sacrifice he had made. She said that she still prayed for him every night. True love never dies.

My heart will forever go out to the 55,573 families, with young wives and loving parents whose hope was shattered by the knowledge that they had lost a precious part of their lives that could never be replaced.

I have had the most incredible life and I thank the Lord that even at the age of 95, I still haven't found that other shoe! Perhaps the next time I climb those stairs I will be granted entry through those gates for a reunion with all those good friends lost so long ago.

In the early stages of the war Winston Churchill declared:

> *"Hitler knows that he will have to break us in this island or lose the war......."*

... against all odds - Great Britain did not break!

Getting ready at the Bomber Command Memorial service, Green Park, London, 28th June 2012.

Meeting His Royal Highness, The Prince of Wales (aka Prince Charles).

A time for reflection and remembrance beside the Bomber Command Memorial in Green Park London.

Bomber Command Memorial unveiling on 28th June 2012.

The UK's last airworthy Avro Lancaster - PA474 - dropping thousands of poppies, during the unveiling of the Bomber Command memorial.

ABOUT THE AUTHORS

JOHN HENRY MELLER

On leaving the RAF in 1950 John joined the Metropolitan Police becoming a Detective Inspector at Scotland Yard. He was involved in cases such as the Kray twins, the Great Train Robbery and many major Post Office and Treasury Department frauds.

At 95 John is currently occupied writing his second book *'On the Beat with Only One Shoe'* with the help of his daughter and co-author Caroline.

ABOUT THE AUTHORS

Caroline Brownbill

Caroline initially trained as a school teacher, obtaining a Bachelor of Education Degree (B.Ed) and working for two years as a primary school teacher. She then switched careers to become an airline pilot and obtained an Airline Pilot Transport Licence (ATPL). She flew commercially for 20 years, finishing her career as an Airline Captain for British Regional Airlines at Cardiff Airport. Caroline says she only became an Airline Pilot because her father John forgot to pick her up from college one day – but that's a whole other story!

She now works full time along with her daughter Stephanie running their own Livery Stables from their small holding in South Wales.

ABOUT THE
ROYAL AIR FORCE
BENEVOLENT FUND

Against the background of writing 'The Boy With Only One Shoe', both of the authors felt it important to highlight the work of The Royal Air Force Benevolent Fund.

The Royal Air Force Benevolent Fund is the Royal Air Force's leading welfare charity, providing financial, practical and emotional support to serving and former members of the RAF – regardless of rank – as well as their partners and dependents.

They help members of the RAF Family deal with a wide range of issues: from childcare and relationship difficulties to injury and disability, and from financial hardship and debt to illness and bereavement. Any member of the RAF Family can approach the Fund for help, which includes serving and former members of the RAF, their partners and dependents.

To find out more about the organisation's work – including how to get involved and how to donate – please visit:

rafbf.org

It is the authors' hope that sales of 'The Boy With Only One Shoe' will allow us to donate to the RAF Benevolent Fund.

Money donated by the authors from the proceeds of this book will be published annually on the website:

JHMeller.com

ACKNOWLEDGEMENTS

Both the authors wish to say a huge thank you to our book designer - Mark Thomas (coverness.com) - for all his expertise and enthusiasm in this project.

Mark is a very experienced book cover, illustrations and interior format designer, but his involvement in this book didn't just stop there. He was determined to make sure we succeeded in publishing this book, as he felt as strongly as we did that this story needed to be read.

Few now remain who are able to give a personal account of what it was like to both live and experience combat during wartime and Mark was as keen as us that this account should be preserved for future generations to share.

Mark thank you for all your knowledge and patience so willingly given. We really appreciate it.

We are also very grateful to Mark for finding us the perfect developmental editor in Claire Sanders (clairesanders.uk). Claire provided thorough editorial guidance on John's account, whilst still remaining sensitive to the very personal nature of the story. Thank you, Claire!

JOHN HENRY MELLER & CAROLINE BROWNBILL
- MAY 2020

APPENDIX A

Aircraft Refernces

Aircraft in which John operated during his RAF career included:

Avro Anson
Avro Lancaster
Avro Lincoln
De Havilland Dominie
Percival Proctor
Vickers Wellington

Other aircraft mentioned in the book and operated by the RAF:

De Havilland Mosquito
Hawker Hurricane
Short Sunderland
Supermarine Spitfire

American aircraft:

Boeing B-17 Flying Fortress

Boeing B-29 Superfortress

German aircraft:

Folke-Wulf Fw 190

Heinkel HE 177

Messerschmitt Bf 109

Zeppelin airship

Japanese aircraft:

Mitsubishi A6M Zero

APPENDIX B

Other Pilots

Although I mainly flew with Squadron Leader Rogers throughout the duration of World War 2, I also flew with many other pilots, particularly after the war had ended. The names of the 82 pilots I flew with are listed below:

AIR COMMODORE
Kirkpatrick OBE

GROUP CAPTAIN
Bachelor CBE DFC

SQUADRON LEADERS

Rogers

Payne

Baker

Blount

Foster

Hamilton

Brooks

WING COMMANDERS

Chilton

Macfarlane

Monroe

Lyster

PILOT OFFICER

Mintor

Detheux

FLIGHT LIEUTENANTS

Wheeler

Lowe

Mathers

Betson

Blair

Facey

Watts

FLIGHT LIEUTENANTS (contd.)

Cook

Scott

West

Chopping

Beech

Graham

Wilson

Perry

Williams

Bull

Castagnola

Cousins

Marwick

Butlers

Baird

Pozzozica

Neubroch

Roberts

Tracey

FLYING OFFICERS

Armstrong

Mather

Bacon

Rignall

Shaw

FLYING OFFICERS (contd.)

Shadwell

Cheek

Baker

Perkins

Wyche

Ansell

Darlow

Woodcock

Gibbons

WARRANT OFFICERS

Potter

Flurley

Edmonds

PILOTS

Balcombe

Kidd

Greenhead

Stanford

Higgins

FLIGHT SERGEANTS

Bell

Wilding

Roddie

Sullivan

FLIGHT SERGEANTS (contd.)

Tosney

Moore

Cook

Garner

Campbell

SERGEANTS

Scott

Jackson

Sovram

Scott

Grannell

Fitzgerald

Bryan

Brooks

Rimmer

Yates

Fisher

The ranks are as recorded in my logbook. However, many of the pilots may have subsequently been promoted.

Printed in Great Britain
by Amazon